The Twenties

An illustrated
History in colour
1919-1929

By
R J Unstead

Macdonald Educational

2

Introduction
The Twenties

Contents

4 **The Shattered Continent**
6 **The Roaring Twenties**
8 **Civil War in Russia**
10 **Aviation**
12 **Labour Unrest**
14 **American Society**
16 **Gandhi's Fight for Freedom**
18 **Mussolini in Italy**
20 **Cars**
22 **The Middle East**
24 **The Arts**
26 **The Ruhr Takeover**
28 **The Munich Putsch**
30 **Sport**
32 **Russia in the Twenties**
34 **Science in the Twenties**
36 **Popular Entertainment**
38 **China and Japan**
40 **Moving Pictures**
42 **Gangsters and Prohibition**
44 **The Birth of Broadcasting**
46 **Colonial Empires in Africa**
48 **The Wall Street Crash**
50 **Reference Section: Literature in the Twenties**
52 **The Main Events: 1919-29**
54 **Who Was Who**
56 **Project: Model Cars**
58 **Project: Record Charts**
60 **Project: Crystal Set**
62 **Index**
64 **Further Reading**

© **Macdonald Educational Ltd.**
Macdonald & Co. (Publishers) Ltd.
Maxwell House, Worship Street,
London EC2A 2EN

Hardback Edition
First published 1973
Reprinted 1974, 1982, 1983
ISBN 0 356 04092 5
Library of Congress Catalog Card No. 72-92429

Printed in Great Britain by
Purnell & Sons (Book Production) Ltd.
Paulton, England

The nineteen-twenties have become a legendary decade. This was the era of jazz and the Charleston, of short-skirted, bob-haired young women beginning to compete with men for jobs. New pleasures became available to almost everyone—the cinema, radio, popular sport, dance-halls and motor-cars. It was as if people were making up for the misery of war by enjoying themselves as hectically as possible.

But the efforts of the Bright Young Things to shock their elders were far less shocking than the reality of the post-war world. A brief boom was followed by mass unemployment; strikes and riots took place in most industrialized countries; German money became virtually worthless for a while, and German coalfields were occupied by French troops; Communism triumphed in Russia and Fascism in Italy, while American gangsters fought out their private wars. Nevertheless, by 1929, hopes for peace and prosperity were growing brighter when the New York stock market collapsed and the whole world slid into the Great Depression.

◁▷**Contrast in the twenties:** the returned soldier comes home to the misery of unemployment while the rich display the latest fashions at the races.

The Shattered Continent

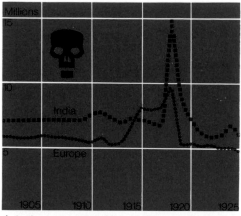

△ **In the years 1918-19, an influenza epidemic** swept across the world from America to China, killing far more people in a few months than the war had done in four years. 27 million are reckoned to have died. The graph above shows death figures in millions for Europe and India, 1900-25.

▽ **War in Ireland:** British soldiers during the bitter fighting of 1919-21, when the Irish challenged British rule. By the 1922 Treaty, Ireland was partitioned into the Irish Free State and Northern Ireland, but this settlement was followed by civil war between Irishmen who supported the treaty and those who wanted independence for the whole of Ireland.

When the twenties opened, Europe was still suffering from the effects of war. It could not have been otherwise. Millions had died in the fighting; millions more had perished from disease and hunger.

The four great empires of Austria-Hungary, Germany, Russia and Turkey had collapsed; while new governments in a score of countries tried to make democracy work, the old trust in authority and discipline had broken down.

France, Belgium and Poland had suffered terribly. In France alone, the Germans had destroyed three million houses, besides factories, mines, bridges and railways. They had removed livestock and ruined millions of acres of farmland.

Poland had been the eastern battlefield and its brave people, eager for revenge, had rashly invaded Russia only to have their country overrun by Bolshevik forces. Pilsudski and the French saved them and the Poles turned with little success to the business of governing themselves.

In Germany, the extreme left wing had tried to stage a revolution but the Army High Command stood firm and when it became clear that the German people were not in a revolutionary mood, the old officer class and the country's conservative forces reasserted themselves. The Kaiser had departed and a moderate Socialist government was formed, but power rested in the hands of officials and regular officers. In 1920 occurred the Kapp putsch, an attempt by anti-republicans to seize control, but although this failed, it was clear that right wing violence had its friends.

There was violence, too, in Hungary where Bela Kun set up a Communist régime which was speedily replaced by an anti-Bolshevik government. All over Europe, statesmen dreaded the spread of Bolshevism. In Moscow the Communist International had been founded and Communist parties had been established in almost every western democracy.

Yet, so far, the Bolsheviks made little progress in the new states created by the peace treaties. In Finland, the Reds were crushed by government troops but a more powerful deterrent was the dividing up of the great estates among the peasants who, as landowners, wanted independence, not Communism.

France, drained to the point of exhaustion, was determined to make the Germans pay for the damage they had done and the realization that Germany was hungry, troubled and equally exhausted only intensified the French demands.

Britain, despite her losses in men, money, and shipping, was perhaps the most stable of the European countries, yet troops had to be used to quell disorder during strikes in Glasgow, and militant trade unionists were demanding a better deal for the workers. The post-war boom was over, and unemployment rose to over two million.

△ **A German Spartacist poster** showing a fist smashing the German parliament. In 1918 soldiers and sailors mutinied, setting up Workers' and Soldiers' Councils in imitation of the Russian Bolsheviks. A left-wing group called the Spartacists tried to stage a revolution, but this fizzled out.

◁ **British ex-servicemen** about to go on the streets as hawkers. Post-war prosperity lasted for about a year; then came massive unemployment, so that men like these tried anything to make a living.

△ **Misery in Berlin:** civilians and demobilized soldiers in the German capital after the end of the war. The Allied blockade had brought near-starvation and the Germans now had to endure unemployment, strikes, street violence and the humiliation of defeat. They bitterly resented being blamed for the war.

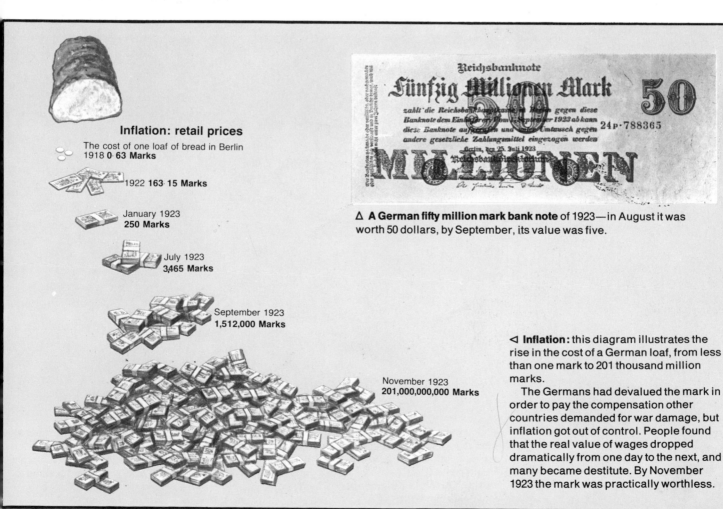

Inflation: retail prices

The cost of one loaf of bread in Berlin
1918 0·63 Marks

1922 163·15 Marks

January 1923
250 Marks

July 1923
3,465 Marks

September 1923
1,512,000 Marks

November 1923
201,000,000,000 Marks

△ **A German fifty million mark bank note** of 1923—in August it was worth 50 dollars, by September, its value was five.

◁ **Inflation:** this diagram illustrates the rise in the cost of a German loaf, from less than one mark to 201 thousand million marks.

The Germans had devalued the mark in order to pay the compensation other countries demanded for war damage, but inflation got out of control. People found that the real value of wages dropped dramatically from one day to the next, and many became destitute. By November 1923 the mark was practically worthless.

The Roaring Twenties

The passage of time has invested the twenties with their own glamour and we can now see that many of our freedoms and pleasures had their origins in this period.

What were the causes of this eruption of gaiety? Partly, it was a reaction against the war years and the gloom of the post-war world. A great many people had done very well out of the war and in some quarters of society there was plenty of money with which to cut a dash.

Women who had worked in wartime factories were not going back to subservience, to ankle-length dresses, and woollen stockings. They could find jobs now in offices and industries where machinery had reduced dependence on manual labour. Professions started to open their doors to middle-class girls who had attended universities, and even married women found greater independence, now that families were smaller owing to birth-control. The "Bright Young Things" of smart society set the style by shocking their elders with their cocktail parties and nightclubs; young women cropped their hair, wore outrageously short skirts, smoked cigarettes and used lipstick.

The craze for dancing spread to all classes and the visit to the cinema became a regular weekly jaunt. The new independence and gaiety of women was in some ways a demand for male attention, for the war had left a large surplus of young women over young men.

Of course the wild goings-on of the smart set were not shared by the great majority of citizens. Nevertheless, there was undoubtedly a general desire for more pleasure and entertainment in the lives of ordinary people.

◁ **Competitors in a Dance Marathon,** nearing exhaustion after 40 hours. They would dance nonstop until all but the winning couple had literally fallen out. These marathons, held mostly in America, attracted poor young people who needed the prize money.

△ **Jubilant "flappers",** rejoicing at possession of the vote, surround a Conservative candidate for Parliament. In Britain, women over 30 were given the vote in 1918, but ten years passed before everyone over 21 could vote. Young women were known as "flappers".

△ **A glamorous advertisement for a motor-car.** Until the twenties, only the rich could afford cars, but, in America, Henry Ford brought them within reach of the ordinary man, and Britain followed suit with Austin Sevens and Morris Minors. France produced the cheap Citroen.

△ **A bathing beauty** in the arms of the law in Chicago while another is arrested on the sidewalk. One-piece bathing-costumes which revealed the female shape were banned by law in some American States, just as bikinis and mini-skirts have been banned in some countries in recent times.

△ **Society women learning the Charleston,** one of the new dances which caught on like wildfire. Others were the Black Bottom and the Heebie-Jeebies. Every smart hotel had its dance floor and dance halls were opened everywhere.

◁ **What the smart world was wearing** in the mid-twenties: Paris fashions as revealed in an English magazine of 1925. Notice the "shingled" hair style of the women, the sleek-headed men in immaculate evening suits, the uneven hems of the loose, low-waisted, backless dresses. Paris was traditionally smarter and gayer than London; it dictated fashion and its night-clubs and cabarets were more daring than any, except perhaps those of Berlin.

Civil War in Russia

For several years after the Revolution in Russia, the Bolsheviks seemed unlikely to survive. Enemies rose up on every side and a bitter Civil War broke out.

△ **A Russian poster** shows a Red soldier bayonetting a Polish landlord—but the Poles nevertheless drove the Russians out.

Their hatred of Russia was deep-seated and Pilsudski had popular support when, taking advantage of the Bolsheviks' difficulties, he invaded the Ukraine.

In 1917 Lenin's Bolshevik party emerged as the best organized and most ruthless of all the revolutionary groups. Lenin made a costly peace with Germany, in order to consolidate the revolution at home, but new enemies now took the field.

Anti-revolutionaries of every kind, known as the Whites, began to challenge the Bolsheviks' authority. These included people who wanted to restore Tsarism, moderates, and Socialists who wanted a more democratic form of government than that proposed by the Bolsheviks. Regional groups like the Ukrainians, the Balts and the Cossacks formed White armies and joined the anti-revolutionaries, enlisting support among the richer peasants who were afraid that the Bolsheviks would confiscate their property. Lenin's government found itself threatened from north, south, east and west.

The Whites were assisted by Russia's former allies. The British, French and Americans had been shocked by Lenin's peace with Germany, and had helped Russian opponents of Bolshevism in the hope that they would bring Russia back into the war. After Germany's defeat, the Allies continued to support the Whites with arms, equipment and troops. The Japanese, hoping to gain from the chaos in which Russia found herself, also sent a force. But Allied intervention was half-hearted; Allied politicians knew that their war-weary peoples would not stand for massive intervention.

The Poles, working off half a century of grievance against Russia, launched a more damaging attack; but now that the Whites were allied with foreign powers, Lenin could appeal to Russian patriotism in defence of the Bolshevik state.

Trotsky, Lenin's most powerful colleague at this time, built up the Red Army, and one by one the White forces were defeated. Their weakness was that they lacked a common policy to appeal to the Russian masses. The peasants, in particular, knew that victory for the Whites would mean a return of the landlords. So, despite civil war and foreign intervention, Bolshevism survived in Russia.

By 1920, the White leaders Kolchack and Denikin were defeated. Pilsudski, the Polish leader launched an invasion and captured Kiev in the Ukraine, only to be swept back almost to Warsaw by the Red Army. However, with French help, the Poles drove the Russians back, and peace was concluded.

◁ **Red sailors go into action** against the White army of General Yudenich who came close to capturing Petrograd (Leningrad) during the Civil War. The Bolsheviks introduced compulsory military service, and a Revolutionary War Council to direct their armies.

△ **Polish cavalry** charging in one of the battles of 1920 against the Russians. The Poles counter-attacked and drove on past the Curzon Line which was to mark their eastern frontier.

The Allies saw, in Poland, a barrier to the spread of Bolshevism, for the Poles, ardent patriots and Catholics, regarded Russians with hatred and contempt.

△ **Rail-travel during the Civil War** in Russia where the transport system was in chaos after continuous fighting since 1914. Trains were so rare that troops and civilians rode on the top of carriages and anywhere they could get a foothold.

△ **Map** showing the extent of 18th-century Poland (which was dismembered by Russia, Austria and Germany) and the red line marking the borders agreed by the 1921 Treaty of Riga with Russia.

△ **Josef Pilsudski,** who, as a youth, suffered in the cause of Polish independence and in 1914 fought for the Austrians. When his country was resurrected in 1918, he became its President and tried to restore "Greater Poland".

Aviation

The war had proved the military value of the aeroplane, and the twenties saw the growth of civil aviation and of pioneering flights across the world.

At the end of the war, many pilots were eager to prove that flying could provide an efficient passenger service, but so far, very few airfields existed. There were no civil aircraft, so the pioneer flights had to be made in converted bombers.

In 1918, some British officers flew in a series of hops to Cairo and India, and, in the following year, two others, Alcock and Brown, made the first non-stop crossing of the Atlantic in a Vickers Vimy bomber. Then, Captain Ross Smith reached Australia in 27 days, Lieutenants Kelly and Macready flew non-stop across the United States in 1922, and, in 1924, two Douglas biplanes flew round the world in 15 days.

The world's first regular air service began in 1919 when a bomber flew from London to Paris with one passenger and a consignment of goods and mail. The Dutch K.L.M. Airline started in this year and in Britain, where civil aircraft began to be built, several airlines were formed. By 1924, these were amalgamated into Imperial Airways. Curiously enough, scheduled passenger services did not start in the United States until 1927.

Throughout the twenties, long distance airmen like Alan Cobham, Kingsford Smith, Byrd and Hinkler pioneered the world's air routes, so that, by 1929, all the continents and oceans had been spanned by air.

◁ **Charles Lindbergh,** the American pilot whose solo crossing of the Atlantic in 1927 made him world-famous. He flew his single-engined Ryan monoplane from New York to Paris.

△ **The German** *Graf Zeppelin* which flew round the world in 1929, and the **British R101** which crashed on its maiden flight. Airships went out of favour owing to a series of accidents.

△ **Stunt flying in a de Havilland Moth,** one of the sturdy little biplanes which cost less than £600 in the twenties. "Air circuses" used to tour Britain, putting on shows of stunt flying and offering cheap joy-rides to those who dared to take to the air. These circuses helped to make the public air-minded.

◁ Crowds on London's Westminster Bridge watch **Alan Cobham preparing to land his de Havilland DH 50** on the River Thames in October 1927.

Cobham had just become the first man to complete the 26,000-mile round trip to Australia, a landmark in aviation history. During the flight, his mechanic was killed and his plane forced down in the sea.

◁ **Airmail** brought by motor-cycle is about to be loaded on board a de Havilland biplane belonging to Aircraft Transport and Travel Ltd., the company which started the world's first regular civil air service. It operated between London and and Paris, taking two and a half hours, provided there was no emergency landing! Fares cost £15 to £20.

Another early cross-channel service was operated by Handley Page Ltd., a company which also built many of the first civil aircraft.

Labour Unrest

This was a period of labour unrest in most industrial countries. Strikes and riots occurred in France, Italy, Germany, Britain, Japan and the United States.

▽ **Miners leaving the pit:** British miners took the lead in militancy. They were bitterly aggrieved over lower wages and the government's refusal to nationalize the mines.

Although Bolshevism was widely blamed for the troubles and Communist parties were active everywhere, the vast majority of workers were more interested in higher wages and better conditions than in political ideas. In many countries, ex-servicemen had come home to find little improvement in social conditions.

In Britain there was an acute housing shortage, prices had doubled and were continuing to rise. After a brief boom, a slump set in, unemployment soared and those who had work often found their wages cut and hours lengthened.

Discontent was expressed in bitter labour disputes. During the war, labour was scarce and wages had risen. The British unions had gained strength and were determined not to lose ground. Feeling was strongest among the miners. By 1921, coal prices had dropped disastrously and the mine-owners proposed cuts in pay. The miners wanted nationalization of the pits and looked for support to the railwaymen and transport workers. Their allies, however, felt obliged to desert them.

The British Trade Union movement went through a bad time in the twenties, trade and heavy industry declined, wages were reduced, unemployment rose and, after the failure of the General Strike, union membership fell away.

△ **German poster** promising to free workers from Communist shackles. Industrial unrest created widespread fear of a Red takeover.

◁ **Alfred Hoffman** (third left) of the United Textile Workers Union, photographed during a strike in Tennessee in 1929. American union leaders like Hoffman would go about accompanied by an armed bodyguard, for strikes and workers' demonstrations were often broken up by police and militia.

The twenties were prosperous years in the United States, output increased at a tremendous rate and wages were the highest in the world, but there was vast inequality between the rich and the workers. Trade Unionism was generally weak and the workers were far less organized than in Britain or France.

△ **A. J. Cook,** secretary of the British Miners' Federation, addresses a meeting of strikers. This fiery little Communist passionately denounced the injustice of cutting wages and he coined the miners' cry of "Not a penny off the pay, not a minute on the day!"

◁ **Armoured cars in a London street during the General Strike of 1926.** A proposal to cut miners' wages caused the Trade Union Congress to call a general strike in sympathy. For nine days in May, Britain came near to a standstill but the strike failed because the government had prepared emergency plans and called on volunteers to run transport. Strikers and their families were hard hit by loss of wages and union leaders were not prepared to go on when told the strike was illegal. The miners themselves, abandoned by their friends, stayed out for weeks.

American Society

△The anarchists, Sacco (right) and Vanzetti; in 1920, these two poor Italian immigrants were brought to trial for murder. Although no conclusive evidence was brought against them, and the trial was conducted in a scandalous manner, Sacco and Vanzetti were found guilty and executed in 1927.

The seven-year case aroused furious indignation all over the world. Sympathy for the accused was increased by their quiet dignity and humility throughout the ordeal.

America in the twenties presented a picture of extremes, of prosperity and poverty, of freedom and intolerance.

By 1921, Americans had turned their backs on Europe. They had rejected Woodrow Wilson's dream that they should take on world leadership and sort out the troubles of a ruined Europe. What America wanted was a return to "normalcy", to the task of building a free and prosperous society. "The business of the United States is business," declared President Coolidge.

And business boomed in the twenties. Income per head increased by a quarter; prices came down and wages went up, so that luxuries like cars, refrigerators and radios became necessities. This was the era when hire-purchase became commonplace, when skyscrapers changed the skyline of American cities, when films, jazz, sensational newspapers and the dramas of Prohibition added to the excitement of life. For many Americans, theirs was a society based on freedom and equality of opportunity.

The truth was different. Prosperity did not reach everyone and sixty per cent of American families could barely afford the necessities of life. Farming was terribly depressed by falling prices and, in areas like West Virginia, malnutrition was widespread; the South remained poor and backward, while public life was tainted by recurrent scandals about corrupt deals concerning liquor permits and government oil reserves.

An ugly feature of the times was intolerance of minorities and of unorthodox ideas. A Red scare led to a witch hunt for Communists and anarchists, to persecution of unions and the hysteria of the Sacco-Vanzetti trial. Johnny Scopes, a teacher in the state of Tennessee, was prosecuted for teaching the theory of evolution and, more hateful, there was a revival of the Ku Klux Klan which harried Jews and Catholics as well as blacks. America's "open door" policy was abandoned to reduce immigration from southern and eastern Europe, so that, by 1929, only 150,000 aliens were permitted to enter the country.

△ Bessie Smith, the greatest blues singer of the twenties, and perhaps of all time. The blues was a form of singing that grew up among the black population of the United States, expressing the joys and sorrows of a people freed from slavery but still far short of equality. The blues, like jazz, acquired great popularity in the twenties, and provides the basis of much popular music today.

Bessie Smith, "Empress of the Blues", was a major record star in her time. She was to die tragically after a car accident, having been refused admission to an all-white hospital.

△ A Klu Klux Klan initiation ceremony. The hooded Klansmen, with their weird ceremonies and titles, such as Imperial Wizard, Grand Dragon, Kludd and Kligrapp, terrorized black people, Jews, Catholics and foreigners.

In 1923 they exerted such influence that a Catholic candidate for the Presidency was defeated by Klan agitation. By the end of the twenties, however, they were in decline.

△ **Dancers in a night-club swing to jazz:** from a painting by the German artist, Otto Dix, *Large Towns*. The improvised negro music gave the decade its name—the Jazz Age. Starting in New Orleans before the war, and moving up to Chicago, jazz swept the world in the twenties. Its hectic and unfamiliar rhythms were well suited to the changing pace of life.

Jazz also began to bring the problems and vitality of black American culture into the public eye. Though all-white bands were more popular in high society, black musicians like Louis Armstrong and Jelly Roll Morton became celebrities.

15

Gandhi's Fight for Freedom

When and how could the British give self-government to India when it was so deeply divided by race, religion and the caste system?

Until 1919, the British had ruled India pretty well according to the ideals of the Victorians. They dispensed justice and education, maintained law and order and granted Indians an increasing say in provincial government. Indian leaders felt that progress would come through co-operation and persuasion.

By 1919, the situation had changed. Younger men were replacing the moderates and, for them, recently-announced British reforms were not enough; they came too slowly and made no real transfer of power. Agitators provoked riots and the British reacted by making arrests and imprisoning trouble-makers without trial.

At this point, the Indian Congress found an inspired leader in M. K. Gandhi, a brilliant barrister who was both saint and wily politician. Gandhi organized a general strike whilst proclaiming his faith in non-violence; but when crowds gathered and extremists got to work, riots broke out and the shooting began.

Mob violence occurred in Amritsar and when General Dyer, with 50 soldiers, found himself facing a huge illegally assembled crowd, he ordered his troops to fire and 379 Indians were killed. The British government condemned Dyer's action, but the Amritsar Massacre left a stain that could not be wiped away.

Throughout the twenties, Gandhi continued to advocate civil disobedience and to increase his hold on the people's hearts. He went to prison for his activities but, for all his saintliness, India was becoming more troubled than ever. The very prospect of self-rule inflamed the enmity between Hindus and Muslims.

△ **Gandhi** as a young man in South Africa, where he made his name among the Indian population.

△ An Indian peasant ploughing a rice field: India's desperate poverty was partly due to traditional inefficient farming methods. Mechanization was virtually unknown.

△ **A Gandhi badge** worn by his supporters; he ate and dressed like the poorest Indians.

△ **Celebrations on Gandhi Day in Delhi, 1922.** Gandhi was universally revered as a saint, but his political ideas did not always appeal to other Indian leaders. There was much violence despite his pacifist outlook.

He exasperated industrialists by advocating a return to simple village life, and his support for the "untouchables" and appeals to Hindus and Muslims to live together in brotherhood offended strict Hindus.

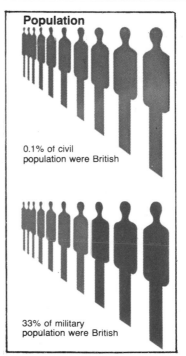

Population

0.1% of civil population were British

33% of military population were British

△ **Diagram** showing how the British, a tiny proportion of the population of India, dominated the army. The Indian soldiers were highly disciplined. At Amritsar it was they who fired on Indian civilians.

△ **British troops in Calcutta** in 1926; they were brought in to quell riots between Hindus and Muslims. Under the British the deep-seated divisions among Indians were held in check, but colonial rule could not be maintained in the face of growing nationalism and resentment.

Mussolini in Italy

Fascism, that evil blight which descended upon Europe during the inter-war years, was born in Italy where Mussolini set himself up as the first of the Fascist dictators.

How did this swaggering bully manage to achieve such mastery over his countrymen? In 1920, Italy was in turmoil; Italians felt that they had done badly out of the war, and d'Annunzio's occupation of Fiume had reawakened dreams of national grandeur. At home, revolutionary agitation led to massive strikes. The weak, divided government seemed unable to cope with threats from Nationalists and Bolsheviks alike, and throughout the country there was poverty and growing unemployment.

Benito Mussolini had been a Socialist at one time, and even edited a Marxist magazine. Impatient with the apparent weakness of the Socialist movement, he formed the first Fascist group in Milan, enlisting other ex-Socialists, students, ex-officers and right-wing malcontents. The Fascists failed to attract much popular support in the Italian elections, and Mussolini turned to other ways of making a name for himself.

He looked for support increasingly among big landowners and industrialists who, in Italy as in so many other countries, were terrified of a Communist takeover. On their behalf, Mussolini organized gangs of Fascist thugs to terrorize the left. The success of these tactics brought new recruits. Army, police, magistrates and politicians thought they could use the Fascists for their own benefit. By October 1922, the month of the March on Rome, Mussolini had found friends all over Italy and was able to bluff his way into office.

By 1925, Mussolini had made himself dictator, with powers to censor the press, radio and cinema, to ban strikes and control the permitted unions. Fascist officials ran the country and Mussolini, "Il Duce", held complete sway.

△ **The Italian poet and nationalist, Gabriel d'Annunzio.** Many Italians wanted Fiume, a port on the Adriatic coast, as a reward for Italy's part in the war. Infuriated by the Allies' refusal to grant it, d'Annunzio and a handful of followers seized the town in September 1919, holding it for over a year before the Italian government—embarrassed by the occupation—forced them to withdraw.

The episode was ridiculous from the start, yet it fired Italian nationalists, and paved the way for Mussolini's equally melodramatic March on Rome.

△ **Army chaplains give the Fascist salute.** The Roman Catholic Church had a powerful influence over the Italian people, so Mussolini decided to win over the clergy by ending the long-standing quarrel between the State and the Vatican.

Though Mussolini never fully trusted the Church, a peace pact made Catholicism the official state religion.

△ **Mussolini and his black-shirted henchmen** parade triumphantly after the March on Rome in 1922. His supporters made the famous march while he came by train!

The March itself was a bluff; designed to overawe the government, it could have been easily crushed by the army. Instead, the King invited Mussolini to be Prime Minister.

▷ **The "Sawdust Caesar" about to address a crowd.** Mussolini (second right) liked to pose in front of the statues that recalled the glory of ancient Rome. The word Fascism itself comes from the Roman symbol of state authority—the "fasces", an axe and bundle of rods. These heroic images in fact contrasted strongly with the shabby reality of Fascism.

Cars

Henry Ford put a cheap popular car on the road as early as 1908, and Americans took enthusiastically to motoring before the 1914-18 War, but, in Europe, it remained a rich man's sport until the twenties.

△ **The British family car** with picnickers at Brooklands race track in 1924. Notice the fold-down windscreen, running-board and tool-box on the open sports model. In 1924, Malcolm Campbell won the world's speed record at Brooklands, doing 146 m.p.h. in a Sunbeam.

The "Tin Lizzie" or Model T Ford was ugly, noisy and bouncy, but it worked and went on working over roads that would appal the modern motorist. Best of all, it was cheap. At $525 or £175 each, Henry Ford had sold a million Tin Lizzies by 1915, and, by 1921, the figure was five million and still rising.

Though Fords dominated the market and had a near-monopoly in countries like Australia, rival models made their appearance and General Motors could offer a choice from among its Buick, Cadillac, Oldsmobile, Pontiac, Chevrolet, Oakland and La Salle cars.

Americans not only had money to buy cars, they also had space to build trunk roads for new vehicles. By the twenties, the country had over 620,000 miles of surfaced roads, whereas Britain constructed only 226 miles of new highway in the decade.

When the war ended, European car manufacturers were mostly small firms (Britain had 96 in 1922), building models one at a time and they doubted if their impoverished countries would take to motoring like the Americans. It seemed safer to stick to the luxury trade and produce cars like the Rolls-Royce, Bentley, Sunbeam, Mercedes and Lancia.

However, in England, W. R. Morris (afterwards Lord Nuffield) began turning out cars by the same kind of mass-production methods as Henry Ford had introduced and, when business fell off, he reacted by *cutting* the price of his cars in order to go on selling. Meanwhile, his rival, Herbert Austin, produced a phenomenally successful baby car, and the French were turning out little Citroens and Peugeots. Designers introduced improvements such as shock-absorbers, four-wheel brakes, dipping headlights and bumpers to make cars safer. Motoring could now be enjoyed by the moderately wealthy, though it still remained beyond the reach of most weekly wage-earners.

The motor-car brought the pleasure of easy travel and touring holidays, along with petrol stations, domestic garages and the spreading of towns into suburbs with ugly ribbon development along main roads. It also brought exhaust fumes, traffic jams and a huge toll of road deaths.

△ **A "bull-nosed" Morris,** one of the best-loved cars ever made, being filled with petrol. Early motorists bought petrol in two-gallon cans from the local ironmonger. They always carried a spare can, for although the first pump delivering petrol from an underground tank was installed in Britain in 1913, roadside pumps were few and far between until well into the twenties.

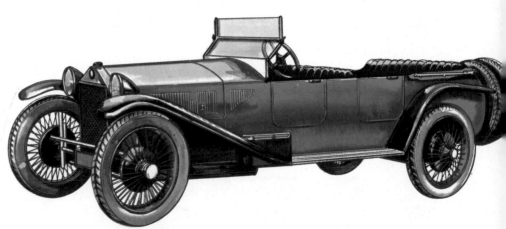

△ **Lancia Lambda, 1925,** an expensive Italian car which could do 70 m.p.h. It had high seats, running-boards, hood and spare wheels at the back. Stream-lining headlamps had not yet been introduced and wings are not fitted into the shape of the body. Motorists wore goggles, helmets and thick leather coats until saloon cars came into production.

△ **Peugeot Quadrilette, 1920,** equipped with electric headlamps and bulb horn, but no front brakes. Light cars seldom had four-wheel brakes. The hood could be folded back and side-screens could be fitted in bad weather.

▽ **Model 'T' Fords** ready for delivery in 1925. They are basically the old Tin Lizzie but the canvas hood has been replaced by a hard top. It was said that the customer could have any colour so long as it was black!

Competition forced Ford to bring out the Model 'A' in 1927, with windscreen-wipers, four-wheel brakes, speedometer—and four colours!

△ **Baby Austin Saloon, 1928,** costing £150. This was a sophisticated version of the original Austin Seven, known as the "Chummy" or, more rudely, as the "Bed Pan", which appeared in 1922, a tiny open tourer, which seated two adults and had a top speed of 38 m.p.h.

The saloon could take three children in the back. Its rival was the Morris Minor, whose price came down to £100.

The Middle East

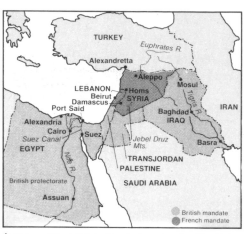

△ **Map of the Middle East,** showing the Turkish provinces which became mandated territories. Mosul, in Iraq, was the centre of rich oilfields and Turkish efforts to recover this province in 1925-6 were frustrated by Britain and the League of Nations.

△ **Turkish bride, wearing the yashmak** to conceal her face from men's eyes. Ataturk made his people adopt Western dress; he emancipated women and gave them the vote.

The breakup of the Turkish Empire gave rise to problems which France and Britain, in particular, could not afford to ignore. Prestige, oil, potential markets, the Suez Canal and growing rivalry between Jews and Arabs kept them involved in the Middle East.

Although Turkey was occupied by Allied troops and invaded by a Greek army, many Turkish officers refused to accept defeat and, under the leadership of Mustafa Kemal (later known as Kemal Ataturk), they raised forces to repel the invaders.

Fighting went on from 1919 to 1922, when Kemal finally drove the Greeks into the sea. He then advanced to Istanbul, whereupon French and Italian troops withdrew, leaving six British battalions to face the victorious Turks at Chanak. Kemal skilfully avoided a major clash and became master of the new Republic of Turkey, which he proceeded to transform into a modern Western State.

There remained the problem of dealing with the former provinces of the Turkish Empire. President Wilson's Fourteen Points had laid down the right to self-determination for all nations and the Egyptians, having got rid of their legal overlord, the Turkish Sultan, naturally thought they would also be rid of their unofficial rulers, the British. But Britain regarded control of the Suez Canal (the key route to India) as essential to her interests and had no intention of giving up her protectorate over Egypt.

Efforts were made in 1922 to frame a Treaty that would give Egypt the outward signs of independence, while the British retained control, an arrangement which King Fuad accepted, but the Wafd or Opposition party, refused. Riots, shootings, and assassination became the order of the day.

As for the rest of the Turkish provinces, the League of Nations decided that these should become mandates, i.e. they should be managed by Allied powers until ready for self-government. Britain was awarded Iraq, Palestine and Transjordan, while France took charge of Syria and the Lebanon. After some initial disorders, affairs in Iraq proceeded far more happily than elsewhere. The British encouraged the Iraqis to take increasing control of their own government; Feisal, the Arab leader, became King and, in an atmosphere of goodwill, the country moved towards complete self-government.

The French were less successful in Syria where, having ejected Feisal, who was King for a time, they proceeded to rule the country as if it were a colony, granting little or no opportunities for unity and independence.

Palestine presented the thorniest problem of all. Here, the British found themselves having to foster a national home for Jews, while trying to appease the Arabs who made up the majority of the population. Jews arrived with Zionist money to buy Arab land and to work towards their cherished aim to found a Jewish state. The Arabs reacted violently and the British became the whipping-boy for both sides. A solution has still not been found for this conflict.

△ **Kemal Ataturk,** the father of modern Turkey, introduces the Latin alphabet to replace Arabic. This greatly helped the spread of literacy.

△ **Mule loaded with products of the Anglo-Persian Oil Company.** The company, which later became British Petroleum, was developing the Middle East oilfields throughout this period.

Desert sheiks suddenly became multi-millionaires, but the people remained poor, and their way of life was not much affected.

◁ **An oil gusher soars hundreds of feet into the air** after an oil strike by the Turkish Petroleum Company in Mosul, Iraq.

This company, mainly a British, French and American concern, was granted concessions throughout Iraq and turned the country into one of the world's major oil-producing areas.

▷ **An Italian poster of the Italian-American Oil Company.** As motoring and industry (especially in countries like Italy which had no coal) demanded increasing supplies of oil, powerful international interests moved into the Middle East to exploit the new-found wealth.

◁ **An early British poster advertising Shell petrol.** Britain had more than a political interest in making a success of her mandate in Iraq. Oil was essential now for transport and defence and its discovery in the Middle East gave imperial powers a new interest in the area.

The Arts

Art, music, literature and architecture took on new and more daring forms in the twenties. Yet the desire to shock, to break away from tradition, was not new in itself and many of the innovations had their origins in the pre-war period.

Paris and Berlin were bursting with creative energy and audacious ideas. Paris, in particular, was a magnet which drew artists and writers from all over the world.

In Germany, despite the oppressive burden of defeat and war guilt, young people were filled with vitality. Schools were run on remarkably progressive lines. In the Bauhaus at Weimar, for example, students were encouraged to break down barriers between art and industrial technology. German architects designed houses and public buildings in revolutionary ways; furniture and interior fittings became starkly functional.

The theatre was supreme in Berlin where Reinhardt put on brilliant productions, while Brecht's *Threepenny Opera*, accompanied by the haunting music of Kurt Weill, disturbed people with its bitter attack on corruption and hypocrisy in society. The mood of bitterness was echoed in German films of the period, and directors like Lang and Weine used the cinema more as an art form than as entertainment.

The most striking innovation in Western art was surrealism, a movement which developed out of the destructive anti-art, known as Dadaism, of the pre-war years. Surrealism was more constructive, and painters like Dali and Ernst used a realistic style to explore grotesque situations from the subconscious mind. There was a nightmarish quality about their work; Dali, for example, would paint a limp clock or a solitary bust on a deserted shore or in some petrified landscape. Surrealism influenced other artists like Picasso, and film-makers like Bunuel.

In music, Stravinsky enhanced the reputation he had acquired before the war, and Bartok was experimenting with new structures, but the characteristic music of the era was American jazz. Musicians like Louis Armstrong, King Oliver, Kid Ory and Jelly Roll Morton now reached a wide audience through gramophone records—an increasingly popular medium. George Gershwin's *Rhapsody in Blue* and *An American in Paris* appeared during the twenties presenting jazz in a highly orchestrated form.

△ *Triangular Hour,* a surrealist painting by Salvador Dali, the flamboyant Spanish artist who settled in Paris. His smooth photographic landscapes have an eerie dream-like quality; people were baffled by his pictures—was he a genius or a charlatan?

△ *A Young Lady's Adventure* (1922) by Paul Klee, who abandoned the idea of a subject in art. Starting with a few lines and splashes of colour, a picture would emerge from his creative "pictorial thinking". Its title came last of all.

△ **Abstract painting,** 1920: Mondrian's composition uses rectangles and areas of pure colour. This geometric style, called Neo-Plasticism, influenced architecture and sculpture.

◁ *Leaves and a Shell,* (1927), by Fernand Leger, a French artist who developed a very personal style out of Cubism.

▷ **Model of the Bauhaus,** built in 1925-26. Started in 1919, by Walter Gropius, this school of architecture and design became famous for breaking down barriers between art and science and bringing into design the techniques of engineering.

It was responsible for the smooth functional style which became characteristic of much new building in Germany, and later in the rest of Europe.

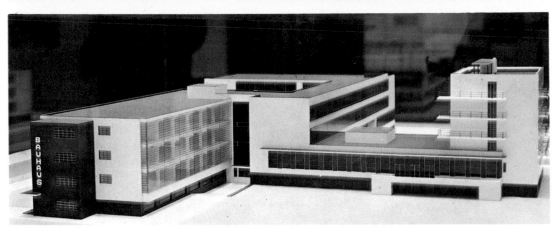

△ **Brass tea and coffee set** designed by Otto Rittweger. Furniture and household objects were as much influenced by the Bauhaus as architecture.

△ **The Red Hot Peppers** playing in Chicago in 1926, with Jelly Roll Morton at the piano. Morton claimed to have "invented jazz in 1901", and although this was an exaggeration, he was probably the most influential jazz pianist, arranger and bandleader of the time.

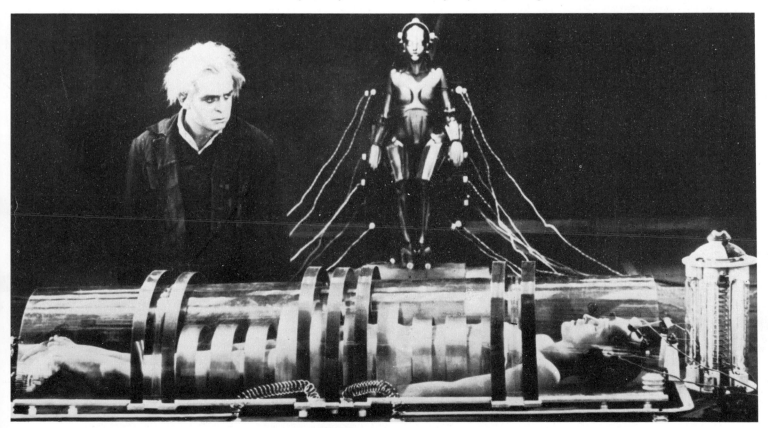

△ **A scene from** *Metropolis,* 1929, directed by the German film-maker Fritz Lang. The film presents a terrifying vision of a city of the future— here a scientist creates a robot. Cinema became a form of art in the twenties; this shot is as carefully composed as a painting.

The Ruhr Takeover

△ **Raymond Poincaré,** the obstinate, patriotic lawyer who expressed the view of every Frenchman in demanding reparations to the full.

Hände weg vom Ruhrgebiet!

△ **"Hands off the Ruhr!"—a German poster** shows France, her hands impaled on chimney stacks, bellowing with pain. The occupation aroused national fury in Germany.

▷ **The Ruhr basin,** showing the extent of the occupation. This was Germany's great industrial area, the key to her recovery and ability to pay reparations. The French believed that the Germans feigned poverty and deliberately caused inflation to avoid paying, but the British thought that Germany would be better able to foot the bill and buy British exports, if she was left to recover in peace.

After the war, Germany had been ordered to meet the cost of making good the Allies' losses. The final figure was colossal, and seemed well above what any country could hope to pay.

Although Britain had given up hope of receiving substantial reparations from Germany, France had not. The trouble about reparations was that no-one was clear on how much Germany should pay. Experts produced all sorts of wild figures and the Germans, though they delivered some coal and coke, became adept at avoiding the payments. The French, who had suffered greatly during the war, believed Germany should not be allowed to escape its commitments, and any politician who expressed doubts on the subject was ousted.

In 1922, Poincaré, an inflexible enemy of Germany, became Prime Minister. Almost immediately, the German Chancellor informed the Reparations Commission that his country could no longer pay. Poincaré's reaction was to order the invasion of the Ruhr in January 1923. Belgian troops joined the French.

The occupation was hotly criticized abroad, especially in Britain, and the Germans themselves were enraged. They resisted the occupiers with strikes and sabotage. Meanwhile, the mark collapsed and German money became practically valueless.

Gustav Stresemann, the new Chancellor of the German Republic, offered conciliation by calling off the sabotage campaign and agreeing to the Dawes Plan of 1924, by which Germany was to pay reparations as her recovery proceeded. At this, the French withdrew. In the following year came the Locarno Pact, guaranteeing the frontiers between Germany and her western neighbours. All seemed set for an era of peace and forgiveness.

▷ **A column of French cyclist troops and armoured cars enter Essen in January 1923.**

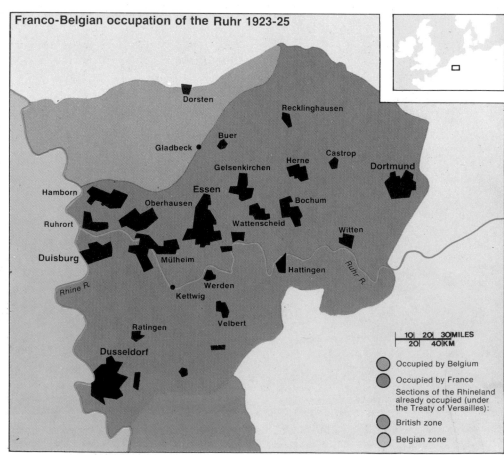

Franco-Belgian occupation of the Ruhr 1923-25

Dorsten
Recklinghausen
Buer
Gladbeck
Castrop
Herne
Gelsenkirchen
Dortmund
Hamborn
Essen
Oberhausen
Bochum
Ruhrort
Wattenscheid
Witten
Duisburg
Mülheim
Hattingen
Ruhr R.
Werden
Rhine R.
Kettwig
Ratingen
Velbert
Dusseldorf

10 20 30 MILES
20 40 KM

Occupied by Belgium

Occupied by France

Sections of the Rhineland already occupied (under the Treaty of Versailles):

British zone

Belgian zone

The Munich Putsch

△ **Gustav Stresemann,** head of the coalition government in 1923, which restored order after the Putsch.

▽ **The accused at Hitler's trial:** Ludendorff in the centre, next to Hitler (in macintosh). Hitler only received a light sentence and, in prison, wrote *Mein Kampf,* setting down the ideas which carried him to power.

The Munich Putsch was a ludicrous failure, but it brought Adolf Hitler into the limelight for the first time.

The Beer Hall Putsch took place on November 8, 1923 in Munich, capital of Bavaria. Its leaders were Hitler and Ludendorff, commander of the German armies in the recent war.

Bavaria had become a centre in Germany for political confusion and often violence. Following the overthrow of the Wittelsbach monarchy in 1918 by a Socialist government, and an attempt to set up a Soviet republic in Munich in 1919, it had become the focus for those who feared renewed Bolshevik activities.

Gustav von Kahr, a right-wing politician, was Bavarian foreign minister 1920-1, and tolerated the spread of para-military groups who opposed Communism, and politicians who regarded the Weimar government in Berlin as dangerously left-wing. Some wanted Bavarian independence and a restoration of the Bavarian ruling family; others hoped to overthrow the republic and establish a dictatorship.

It was during this period that Hitler, then an obscure ex-corporal, joined and became leader of a racialist, nationalistic political group called the German Workers' Party, and later known as Nazis. It had a growing number of sympathizers in the army and in the Munich police; moreover, the Bavarian administration turned a blind eye to the Nazis' violence against Jews, Communists and Republicans in the city.

As a result of the Ruhr occupation and collapse of the mark, relations between Bavaria and Berlin became more strained than ever and when Kahr was billed to address a meeting in a Bavarian beer-hall, Hitler and his storm-troopers decided to take over the meeting and proclaim an uprising.

Ludendorff agreed to join the rebels and he placed himself alongside Hitler as they marched into the centre of Munich. When the authorities narrowly decided against collaboration, armed police faced the marchers and broke their ranks with a few shots. Hitler fled but was arrested and put on trial, where his ravings became headline news. For the moment, he had failed, but his hour would come.

▷ **A Bavarian poster screams, "The Bolshevik is loose!"** With his hand already on Berlin, the dreaded revolutionary is about to destroy Munich. This kind of nationalistic anti-Bolshevik hysteria inspired the Munich Putsch.

BERLIN

MÜNCHEN

BAYERN, DER BOLSCHEWIK GEHT UM!
HINAUS MIT IHM AM WAHLTAG!
BAYERISCHE VOLKSPARTEI

Sport

Sport became big business and increasingly professional. Millions turned out to watch their heroes or listened to radio broadcasts and devoured the sporting press.

△ **Babe Ruth,** the giant of American baseball whose feats with the bat drew enormous crowds and made him the world's most highly paid sportsman. In the twenties, he was the star player of the almost invincible Yankees, hitting a record 60 home runs in 1927.

British soldiers who had enjoyed sport in the Army, came home full of enthusiasm for soccer and, with cheap admission prices, even the unemployed could forget their troubles for a while. The first Cup Final at Wembley in 1923 drew over 120,000 spectators and, at Hampden Park in Scotland, even bigger crowds watched the national game. Soccer was now finding support in Europe and South America, but it never caught on in the United States where baseball and American football held pride of place.

Cricket flourished in England and in most Commonwealth countries, while boxing, horse-racing and car-racing had a much wider international following. Sports like golf and tennis now caught the public's interest and the British, who had originated so many games, had to take a back seat when American golfers like Hagen and Bobby Jones dominated their championships. At tennis, an Australian (Patterson), two Americans (Johnson and Tilden) and three brilliant Frenchmen (Borotra, Lacoste and Cochet) took all the Wimbledon singles titles in the twenties.

Something was done at long last to allow more young people to play games, In Britain, the National Playing Fields Association was founded to provide sports fields, and local authorities and industrial firms started to lay out pitches, tennis courts and swimming-baths.

△ **A soccer match between Chelsea and the Arsenal** at Stamford Bridge in the late twenties. At this time, British soccer was supreme and matches against continental teams aroused little interest compared with home internationals and the League and Cup competitions. Players received only a few pounds a week and big transfer fees were unknown.

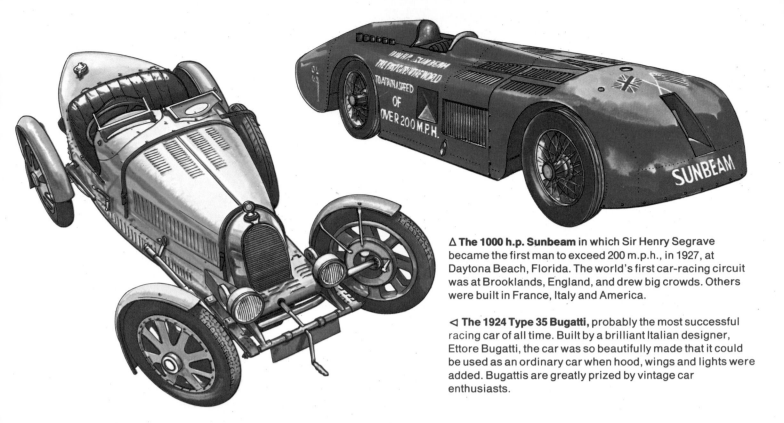

△ **The 1000 h.p. Sunbeam** in which Sir Henry Segrave became the first man to exceed 200 m.p.h., in 1927, at Daytona Beach, Florida. The world's first car-racing circuit was at Brooklands, England, and drew big crowds. Others were built in France, Italy and America.

◁ **The 1924 Type 35 Bugatti,** probably the most successful racing car of all time. Built by a brilliant Italian designer, Ettore Bugatti, the car was so beautifully made that it could be used as an ordinary car when hood, wings and lights were added. Bugattis are greatly prized by vintage car enthusiasts.

△ **Cartoon of Jack Hobbs,** the English batsman who made more runs (61,237) than any other cricketer. He was in top form in the twenties when the County Championships drew big crowds and the Test Matches against Australia eclipsed all other contests. Great cricketers of this era included Hobbs, Sutcliffe, Woolley, Hendren, Duckworth and Freeman, with Macdonald and Gregory, Mailey and Grimmett of Australia.

◁ **Jack Dempsey,** heavyweight champion of the world, is knocked out of the ring by Battling Firpo, in the sensational opening round of a fight in 1923. Dempsey climbed back and knocked out Firpo in the second round. The "Manassa Mauler", as Dempsey was called, was reckoned to be one of the greatest champions, holding his title from 1919 until 1926 when 120,000 spectators saw him beaten by Gene Tunney, an American marine.

Russia in the Twenties

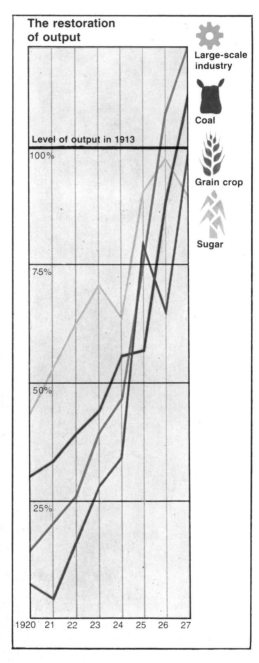

The restoration of output

Large-scale industry

Coal

Grain crop

Sugar

Level of output in 1913

100%

75%

50%

25%

1920 21 22 23 24 25 26 27

△ **Graph showing the recovery of Russian production.** As you can see, the country was in desperate straits in 1920; grain crops amounted to barely one tenth of the pre-war total; industrial output was only one seventh, and coal and sugar had fallen well below half.

Slowly the figures improved, except in 1921, when drought further reduced the harvests. It was 1927 before manufacturing, coal and grain production reached pre-war levels.

By the end of 1920, the Bolsheviks were master of devastated Russia. Lenin, Trotsky and their followers had to rebuild the stricken country, while keeping power in their own grip.

The Bolshevik Party had triumphed through ruthless application of "war Communism". The Party alone ruled the state, and the state supervised production and requisitioned the food needed by the towns. But there were other left-wing parties bitterly hostile to the Bolsheviks who, they thought, had abandoned the fine ideals of the October Revolution.

In 1921, Lenin and Trotsky had to crush a rising of the Baltic sailors in the naval fortress of Kronstadt, where the sailors demanded free elections, free speech and the abolition of terrorism and favouritism—none of which was acceptable to the Party in power.

However, the Kronstadt Rising and the 1921 famine convinced Lenin that he must trim his sails. The peasants, in particular were not ready for all-out Communism, so he produced the New Economic Policy (N.E.P.), allowing them to sell surplus produce and to deal with private traders. This was a risky move, but it worked and production began to recover.

Lenin died in 1924, leaving no clear direction for a successor. Stalin, secretary of the Party, sat at the heart of power, in a position to manipulate elections to the *Politburo* (inner council). He was able to isolate Trotsky and eventually to drive him into exile. By 1927, Stalin was ready to eliminate all his opponents and to don Lenin's mantle as ruler of the Soviet Union. He proved to be more ruthless than Lenin. His Five-Year Plan (1928) was intended to industrialize Russia and to collectivize the farmlands, and those who resisted its aims were wiped out.

△ **Communist posters** designed to convince the peasants that collectivism was better than farming on their own. Here we have three simple peasants, one with a horse, one with a plough (or drill) and one with a bag of seed corn. Separately, none can work his land properly.

△ Now the three peasants can get together to discuss their problems and the outcome is obvious: the horse is harnessed to the machine and the seed is scattered on the land.

△ **A Russian stamp** commemorating the All-Russian Agriculture and Domestic Industry Exhibition 1923, when production was still desperately low. The stamp shows an early farm tractor.

◁ **Lenin talks to aggrieved peasants,** listening to their complaints and sometimes putting them right. The ruthless revolutionary had a kindlier side to his nature; he enjoyed company, lived simply and liked to feel that he was in touch with the common people in the streets and factories. He disliked the personality cult that was built up around him.

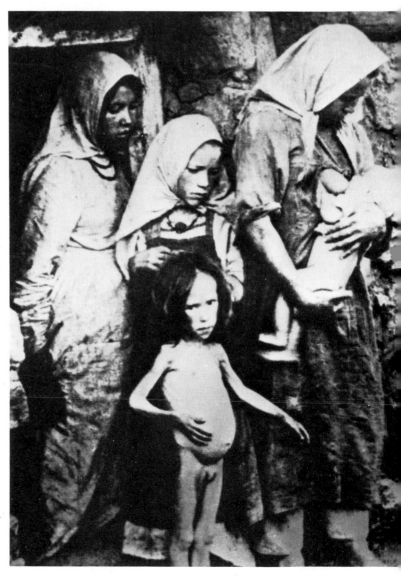

A Bolshevik poster, one of many distributed throughout Russia during 1921: in saying "Remember the starving!", it asks Russians to send food and seed corn to the disaster areas.

△ **A starving family in 1921;** prolonged drought caused harvests to fail over wide areas and more than a million Russians died of hunger. Help came from abroad, particularly from the International Red Cross.

Science in the Twenties

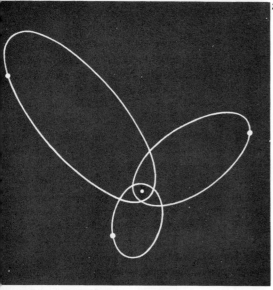

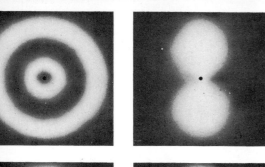

△ **Fig. 1** shows Newton's idea of what atoms looked like. **Fig. 2** represents electrons orbiting a nucleus (the view of the atom at the beginning of this century) and **Fig. 3** shows how modern scientists see four atoms, each with a nucleus and a "probability cloud" where electrons may be found.

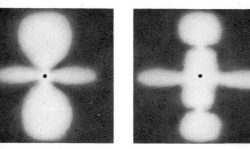

In the twenties, a group of scientists called atomic physicists were keen to discover exactly what the world was made of. It was the Ancient Greek thinker Democritus who had first put forward a theory to solve the problem.

He noticed that there were dips in the steps leading up to the temple where people had walked on them. He concluded that minute pieces of the steps had been worn away and that objects could be made of tiny invisible particles. He called these particles "ATOMS".

Today we believe atoms are so tiny that many millions of them could fit across the full stop at the end of this sentence. For this reason it is difficult to find out what they are really like; the pictures on this page are only drawings of scientists' ideas about atoms.

After the Greeks, scientists for many centuries worked with the idea that everything is built from atoms, picturing them as tiny, indestructible particles.

Newton, at the end of the seventeenth century, held this "classical" view of atoms, when he described them as tiny, hard balls (see picture no. 1).

Rutherford

But in 1911, Ernest Rutherford, working in England, showed that an atom was mostly empty space, and that the weight of the atom was concentrated in a small "NUCLEUS" at its centre.

Two years later, Niels Bohr, a Danish scientist, suggested that the nucleus had a positive electrical charge and that much smaller "ELECTRONS", which had a negative electrical charge, circled round the nucleus like planets in orbit round the sun (picture no. 2).

In 1919 Rutherford showed that the tiny nucleus could be split into smaller particles called "PROTONS".

The modern idea of the atom, developed in 1926, keeps the idea of the central nucleus (picture no. 3). But scientists now say that the positions of the electrons cannot be defined exactly. Instead there is an area where the electrons can probably be found, called a "probability cloud".

The four atoms represented here are those of Hydrogen, Oxygen, Carbon and Sodium.

Relativity

Developing alongside these theories about atoms was Albert Einstein's theory of Relativity concerning matter and energy (1905-15). This was the most important scientific theory of the century.

He proved, using mathematics, that material objects, which scientists call matter, could simply disappear, and be converted into energy. This should not be confused with burning or boiling away, because in these processes, the objects are only turned into gases and matter is not actually destroyed.

His theory was crucial to the development of nuclear physics because he predicted that small amounts of matter could change into enormous amounts of energy.

No-one had ever done this, but the theory was proved in 1919 when one of its predictions—that star-light passing near the sun would be deflected, or bent—was observed during an eclipse of the sun.

However, it was not until 1932 that the first scientists (Cockcroft and Walton) managed to change matter into energy. They succeeded in splitting a big atomic nucleus into two smaller ones. The weights of the smaller nuclei did not add up to the weight of the bigger one. The remainder had turned into energy.

If enough big atoms are split up at the same time, so much energy is released that there is an explosion. This is how the nuclear bomb works (and also why it is called the *atomic* bomb).

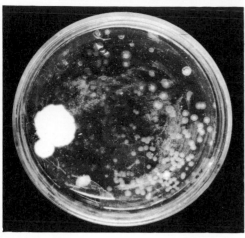

◁ **The mould** growing on the edge of this tray of microbes in 1928 contained penicillin. It was particularly effective in curing gangrene but also cured a wide range of other illnesses, and soon became known as the "wonder drug".

▷ Much of the work in **identifying vitamins** was done in the twenties, but it was slow work because foods only contain tiny amounts of these substances. The discovery of vitamins has made the world a healthier place, and most of the diseases mentioned in this table are almost unknown in many parts of the world today.

Vitamin	Disease caused by deficiency	Foods where found	First identified
A	Night blindness	Liver, fish, animal oils	1920
B	Beri-beri	Cereals	1926
B	Pellagra	Yeast, liver, kidney, milk	1926
D	Rickets	Dairy produce, fish, dripping	1922
E	Sterility, muscular dystrophy	Wheat germ, cereals, corn oil, greens	1922
F	Stops body growth	Vegetables, seed fats, human milk	1929

△ **A photo of Alexander Fleming** in his laboratory during the twenties.

Archaeology

Archaeology attained its coming-of-age during this period when trained, professional archaeologists, using new techniques and a more scientific approach, took over from the enthusiastic amateurs.

The most dramatic of all discoveries occurred in 1922 when Howard Carter, making one final exploration for his patron, Lord Carnarvon, came across the unrifled tomb of the boy-Pharaoh, Tutankhamun. News of the exquisite treasures (which took six years to excavate and catalogue) aroused world-wide excitement and even led to Egyptian-style fashions and decor.

Spectacular finds were also made in Mesopotamia where Sir Leonard Woolley excavated a Sumerian temple and the site of the city of Ur. These excitements tended to overshadow work being done in other parts of the world, as in Central America and Russia where, in 1929, archaeologists found a series of Iron Age Scythian tombs in the permanently frozen earth of Siberia.

△ **The gold mask of Tutankhamun.**

Medicine in the Twenties

Suffering during the First World War inspired doctors and scientists to work hard at finding cures for diseases, and ways of saving life. The decade following 1918 saw some remarkable advances.

The cure for diabetes was found in 1921. Work in Rumania (Nicholas Paulesco) and in Canada (Banting and Best) showed that insulin suddenly made sufferers better. The cure was remarkably simple and the disease is no longer feared as it used to be.

Blood transfusions had become more reliable since 1901, when the importance of not mixing different blood "groups" was recognized. When the British scientist Robertson first succeeded in storing blood (for 21 days) in 1918, by adding glucose to it, the foundations were laid for establishing blood banks.

New techniques were also developed in X-ray photography. Since 1896, when Roentgen discovered X-rays, photographs of the body had shown only the patient's bones. But in 1921 the Frenchman, Bocage, patented a method for making X-ray photographs more sensitive. The internal organs of the body could now be seen much more clearly.

Penicillin

But perhaps the greatest discovery of this period was penicillin—and it was discovered by accident. Alexander Fleming was experimenting with microbes in a tray during the summer of 1928, and left some of these trays unwashed when he went away on holiday.

When he came back, he noticed that mould had started to grow on one of the trays and that this growth had killed off some of the microbes near it. It was this growth, which contained penicillin, which was later tested as an antibiotic and used as a vaccine. It was not until the early 1940s that penicillin was produced in bulk.

Popular Entertainment

△ **Cover of the American magazine** *Life,* April 1923. The discovery of Tutankhamun's tomb gave rise to a mania for everything Egyptian. A whole range of magazines dealing with current affairs, literature and fashion came on the market, some of which, like *Vogue, Time* and the *New Yorker,* still exist.

The rich were still rich, the middle class lived comfortably enough and wage-earners (provided they had work) enjoyed shorter hours and better pay than before the war. So there was an increasing demand for varied entertainment.

Popular newspapers, motor-cars, the cinema, theatre, dancing and holidays had all been available in pre-war days to those who could afford them. By the twenties, most forms of entertainment could appeal to a much wider public.

The motor-car provided a new means of transport for the middle-classes who now enjoyed touring holidays in what had been remote parts of the country. Film-going became a national habit, with over 3,000 cinemas in Britain alone, showing films almost exclusively made in America. The stars of the silent screen—Chaplin, Valentino, Garbo, Fairbanks, Mary Pickford and the rest —were enormously popular and the arrival of the "talkies" in the late twenties made film-going even more entrancing.

The cinema's popularity had an adverse effect on music-halls whose cheerful songs and knockabout comedy seemed out of date compared with the excitement of films. Serious plays were also hard-hit and, in the big cities, successful plays tended to be musicals and sophisticated comedies.

There were more newspapers and literary magazines in the twenties than there are now, with "tabloid" dailies, like the *Daily Mirror* and the *Sketch* in Britain, giving their readers pictures and a livelier presentation of the news. One form of entertainment which became increasingly available in the twenties was radio. In America, broadcasting started in 1920 and two years later from the 2LO station in London. By 1927, over a million people in Britain held radio licences and could enjoy music, talks, plays and comedy in their own homes.

△ **Poster advertising a hand-cream** has a similar Eastern flavour; books and films reflect this passion for the "mysterious East". Advertising was becoming more sophisticated as the persuasion business began to grow into an industry.

△ A French cartoon showing **Charlie Chaplin as the spirit of the cinema,** the "little feller" whom everyone loved. He had developed his style and technique before and during the war, when he appeared in dozens of short comic films. In the twenties, he started to make the full-length pictures which made him the most popular screen actor of all time. His films were silents, and long after the introduction of "talkies", he did not himself speak on film.

△ **Poster advertising a seaside resort.** More people than ever before went on holidays, usually to the seaside. Foreign travel was only enjoyed by the rich. Sun-bathing was the latest craze, now that girls could uncover their legs and backs, though many people thought that the one-piece costumes were shockingly immodest.

▽ **Piccadilly Circus** in the heart of London on a crowded evening in the twenties. Notice the open-topped double-decker buses and the fashions—upper class people going out to dinner or to the theatre wore full evening-dress.

At almost any time, one could be certain that George Bernard Shaw, Noel Coward and Somerset Maugham had plays running in London theatres. Evening entertainments thrived, and in every capital city, central areas grew up to cater for the pleasure-seeking public.

△ **Film-stars at supper in a night-club.** In every capital, the smart set frequented night-clubs which provided meals, dancing and drink at outrageous prices. In Britain, police often raided them for selling drinks after licensing hours and famous hostesses, like Mrs Meyrick, cheerfully paid the fines and even went to prison.

China and Japan

△ **Glorification of violence:** Japanese youths preparing for sport in traditional costume. This reverence for tradition was not confined to the twenties; the military class of old Japan, the *samurai* warriors, were revered and the country's youth was brought up to revere ancestors and practically worship the Emperor. Nevertheless, violence and political murder were never far from the surface.

China had long been plagued by weak and corrupt governments, by the greed of Japan and the Westerners and by her own warlords. In the twenties, China awoke and embarked upon the agonizing struggle to free herself from her enemies.

In 1920, China was in ferment. The last of the Manchu Emperors had been deposed in Sun Yat-sen's 1911 Revolution but the country was still in desperate straits. Its trade was dominated by Western powers, especially Britain; Japan had insinuated herself into the northern territories and the war lords had held sway since 1916. These bandit-generals controlled whole provinces and enriched themselves with murderous greed.

Nevertheless, "Young China" was beginning to stir. This was an idealistic movement of the younger generation who detested the foreigners' domination. They felt that China had been betrayed at Versailles, when Shantung, previously leased to Germany, was awarded to Japan. This provoked the violent revolt of Peking students known as the 4th May Movement of 1919. Chinese Nationalism now came of age; at the same time Chinese Communism was born.

Educated Chinese had seen how the Russians had overthrown a tyrannical régime and then defied foreign intervention. Some Chinese wanted to follow the Bolshevik example, others merely to oust the foreigners and war lords.

Sun Yat-sen tried to unite Communists and Nationalists by forming the People's National Party, the *Kuomintang*. He set up a revolutionary government at Canton, with support from Russia and from the newly-formed Chinese Communist Party whose leaders included Chou En-lai and a young librarian named Mao Tse-tung.

It was an uneasy alliance. Sun Yat-sen's army, led by Chiang Kai-shek, steadily defeated the warlords but the Nationalists and Communists were fighting for different ideals. Sun died in 1925 and was succeeded by Chiang Kai-shek who, like many of his close supporters, came from the landowning class. They were horrified to find that some Communists had encouraged the peasants to take over the land in freed provinces. In 1926 and 1927, Chiang Kai-shek struck savagely at the Communists, killing hundreds and forcing Mao and a few supporters to flee to the mountains when they formed the Red Army and planned their own revolution. By 1928, Chiang Kai-shek was firmly installed as leader of the Republic.

What of Japan during this troubled era? Compared with China, she was strong, prosperous and apparently firmly governed. Japan had done well out of the war; trade and industry had advanced by leaps and bounds and she had acquired big commercial and territorial interests in China, especially in Manchuria.

In the mid-twenties, Japan's leaders pursued a "soft" policy towards China but this was opposed by the powerful Army group which despised politicians and was intent upon annexing Manchuria. The Japanese generals realized that if Chiang Kai-shek united China, their own ambitions would be thwarted.

The growth of Japan

1920   1930

Military Expenditure 123%

Industrial Production 84%

Population 15%

% increase 1930 over 1920

△ **Diagram showing Japan's progress** in the twenties. Money spent on armaments increased at a far greater rate than the population, and industry boomed.

△ **Sun Yat-sen's portrait** on a banknote. Revolutionary and founder of the Kuomintang, he collaborated with Russia and the Chinese Communists, whose aims he found compatible with his own.

◁ **Mao Tse-tung** at the head of peasant forces in 1927, the year of the final split between the Nationalists and the Communists. He fled to Chingkangshan in the mountainous south to raise the Red Army.

△ **Chiang Kai-shek** who succeeded Sun Yat-sen and defeated the warlords. President of the Republic, he unified China but could not break the Communists.

◁ **The Uprising of May 4th 1919:** Peking students urge a boycott of Japanese goods in protest against the Versailles award of Shantung to Japan. The student rising achieved little, except that China refused to sign the Treaty of Versailles, but it awoke Chinese nationalism and intensified hostility to all foreigners.

Mving Pictures

During the war, film-going had become an established habit in America and in Europe. It was an escape from the worries of daily life.

Film production in Europe was disrupted during the war years, leaving the field clear for American producers. California's dry, sunny climate was ideal for outdoor shooting and American business efficiency soon built up chains of cinemas to show the films produced in Hollywood. The Keystone Company made short hilarious films, featuring comedians like Fatty Arbuckle, Chester Conklin and a little Englishman named Charlie Chaplin.

After the war, European producers re-emerged and Eisenstein, a Russian, made a great film *Battleship Potemkin*, and many others with a revolutionary or social theme. The Russian film-makers lacked the resources of the Americans, but they had the advantage of being given the full support of their government.

The star system became firmly estab-lished; there was Theda Bara, a glamorous villainess, Lillian Gish, Mary Pickford, Harold Lloyd, Buster Keaton, Douglas Fairbanks, Valentino, the great lover, and of course Chaplin, who became the biggest box-office draw of them all. The fascinating Greta Garbo arrived in the late twenties.

Silent films created no language barriers, for the short sub-titles could easily be replaced by translations. Nonetheless, the arrival of talking pictures in 1927 was a great technical advance. Some silent stars departed but the ones who took their place could now use a more natural style of acting.

Lavish musicals flourished and became extremely popular, and Walt Disney used sound in the second of his cartoons to feature Mickey Mouse, a character he created in 1928. It became an immediate success.

◁ **Charlie Chaplin** and Jackie Coogan in *The Kid* (1920). Written and directed by Chaplin it was a fabulous success, followed by *The Gold Rush* (1925) and *The Circus* (1928).

△ **Al Jolson** in *The Jazz Singer* (1927), the first "talkie". He became world famous with *The Singing Fool* in which he sang *Sonny Boy,* a song of sickly pathos which became universally popular.

△ **Rudolph Valentino** and his wife, with their Voisin car, in France. An Italian, Valentino specialized in heavily romantic roles. When he died at 31, thousands of hysterical women rioted at his funeral. His major successes were *The Sheik, Blood and Sand, Monsieur Beaucaire* and *The Eagle.*

△ **Filming the chariot race** in *Ben Hur* (1926), one of the many big spectaculars produced in the twenties, starring Ramon Navarro and Francis X. Bushman, and directed by Fred Nilbo.

KEYSTONE
COMEDIES

"La Nouvelle Profession De Charlot"

WESTERN IMPORT Cᵒ Lᵀᴰ
WESFILM HOVSE GERRARD STREET LONDON

△ **Harold Lloyd** in a scene from *Safety Last* 1923). His popularity as a star arose from his hilarious attempts to get out of fantastic predicaments, such as the one in the picture.

◁ **Poster advertising Keystone Comedies** made by Mack Sennet who directed Chaplin in 35 films in 1914, and made him a star. Chaplin however was too independent to stay with Keystone.

Gangsters and Prohibition

On 17th January 1920, all alcoholic drink was banned throughout the United States. Prohibition, as it was called, gave rise to a decade of unparalleled crime and corruption.

△ **Prohibition fashion note:** the "Rum Apron", containing several bottles of liquor, which can be hidden by the long jacket.

Puritanism had never died out in America and the long-standing Temperance movement, headed by the Anti-Saloon League and the Women's Christian Temperance Union, had been encouraged by the wartime restrictions on drinking. Prohibition became law and America suddenly found itself "dry".

The results should have been obvious but the incredible thing was that no-one seems to have foreseen them. Evading the law at once became a kind of sporting compulsion for ordinary citizens, and big business for criminals. Thousands of soft drinks parlours called "speak-easies" opened to sell liquor at inflated prices; illegal brewing became a multi-million dollar industry, with Chicago the centre for liquor production and for the gangsters who controlled its distribution.

So vast were the profits from "bootleg" liquor that police, officials, politicians and even judges were drawn into the network of crime. In four years, 227 gangsters were murdered without one conviction being recorded. It was reckoned that 2,000 civilians and 500 Prohibition agents were killed; figures for drunkenness and drunken driving soared and consumption of alcohol reached astronomical heights. People drank as never before but perhaps the worst aspects of Prohibition were almost universal contempt for law which it bred, and the public's hero-worship of murderous thugs.

An end to this disastrous state of affairs came in December 1933 when Prohibition was repealed. The public had become sickened by the results of an absurd law, but the legacy of corruption was by no means dead.

△ **Prohibition agents break open kegs of bootleg liquor.** A certain amount of alcohol was intercepted and destroyed, but vast quantities still reached a public which was determined to drink.

It proved impossible to enforce a law which millions of people regarded as absurd and tyrannical.

◁ **A German comment on Prohibition:** the cartoon shows Uncle Sam exhausted by the effort of trying to destroy an endless stock of bootleg liquor. It proved impossible for 1,500 Prohibition officers to enforce a law which millions of Americans were determined to evade.

◁ **Al "Scarface" Capone,** most notorious of all the gangsters. Italian by birth, he moved from New York to Chicago as a young man and quickly became head of a bootleg and vice syndicate. He crushed all opposition by ruthless terrorism and was said to have been implicated in 400 murders.

Flashily dressed and driven about in an armour-plated Cadillac, he was known as Public Enemy Number One, but such was his power that no charges of murder were made against him. He was eventually jailed for ten years for tax evasion.

▽ **A girl strap-hanger** lapping up the latest crime story. The violent activities of gangsters became top-line news, sensationalized in the new "tabloid" newspapers.

△ **Funeral of Dion O'Banion,** a Chicago gang leader. 26 truck loads of flowers followed his silver-edged coffin and 20,000 people, including judges and aldermen, attended his funeral.

▽ **Frank Yale,** Mafia chief and liquor boss of New York, lies dead beside his Lincoln car in Brooklyn, 1928. He was machine-gunned to death by order of Al Capone.

The Birth of Broadcasting

Marconi transmitted radio signals as early as 1897. Yet it was another 23 years before broadcast programmes reached people's homes.

△ **A radio van** receiving a political speech and broadcasting it through loud-speakers in 1924. These vans gave politicians a new way of reaching the public, most of whom did not yet have radios of their own.

Radio was originally seen as a means of sending signals without landlines; it was particularly useful for transmitting messages to ships at sea. Although Professor John Fleming's invention of the radio valve made speech transmission possible, the war put an end to experiments in radio *telephony* in Europe. During the war, Army and Navy telephonists tapped out their messages in Morse code.

However, in America, experiments went on and, in 1915, words *spoken* from New York were received in San Francisco. Broadcasting to the public began in 1920 in the United States where over a thousand stations were licensed in the next four years.

Things moved more slowly in Europe. The Marconi Company resumed experiments in Britain and was carrying out transmissions from Chelmsford in 1920, the year when Dame Melba made her historic broadcast. Transmissions lasting an hour each evening, were received mostly by amateurs using

home-made sets and the programmes themselves were distinctly amateur—newspaper extracts, piano solos and so on. Other companies started broadcasting, and commercial radio might have developed as in America and most European countries, had it not been for government action.

In 1922, it was decided that one company, the British Broadcasting Company, should have a monopoly. There would be no advertising but revenue would come from licences on receiving-sets.

The London station, 2LO, moved to Savoy Hill and more professional programmes began to go on to the air. The range was limited, and interference was often bad; however, a high-powered transmitter was built at Daventry so that, with studios in other cities, the whole country was covered. By 1926, over two million licences were issued and "the wireless" (it was not yet called radio) was becoming part of everyone's life.

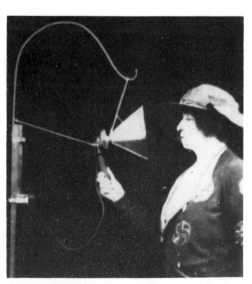

△ **Dame Nellie Melba,** the famous primadonna, about to sing into the microphone in June 1920. She was invited to Britain's first broadcasting station at Chelmsford, and her marvellous voice convinced people that radio had a future as mass entertainment.

△ **John Logie Baird** at work during the B.B.C.'s first experimental television broadcast in 1929. Pioneer scientists had earlier shown that light impulses could be transmitted and received by cathode ray tubes (1908) but little was done until the Scotsman Baird devoted himself to the problem.

By 1920, he had demonstrated radio vision in London and his apparatus was on show at the Wembley Exhibition of 1924. Then came his triumph. In 1928, he transmitted pictures from London to New York. However, it was 1936 before the world's first public television service began operating.

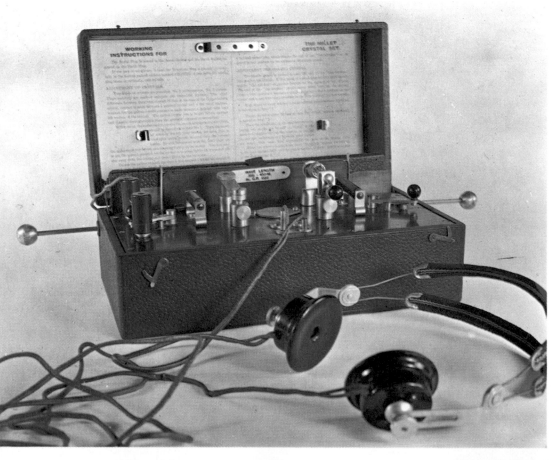

◁ **Millet's crystal radio,** with earphones, 1923. Early sets had no valves but used a crystal-detector (the crystal usually being a thin piece of quartz or carborundum) on which a fine wire rested, called a "cat's whisker".

You had to tickle the cat's whisker to tune in and, as sounds from crystal sets were never very loud, you needed earphones. Several pairs would be provided when guests came to "listen in"

Many sets were home-made, and newspapers carried articles telling enthusiasts how to build their sets, how to erect a pole in the garden for the aerial and the way to make an "earth" by driving a metal pipe into the soil.

◁ **The first Philips all-mains receiver with speaker, 1928.** Until this time, radio sets with valves (replacing the crystal and cat's whisker) required a large dry-battery and an "accumulator" which had to be taken to a shop every week to be re-charged.

▷ **A 1925 Gecaphone battery radio set** with an Amplion speaker. By now, valve sets could use loudspeakers, trumpet-like horns fitted to versions of the telephone earpiece. You can see that the set had a knob which was turned to find the station; another knob moved coils to regulate the sound.

Colonial Empires in Africa

In the twenties, Africa generally was quiet. Colonial powers ruled practically the whole continent; there were few upheavals and scarcely a mention of independence or African nationalism.

Except in Morocco and Egypt, there was no active resistance to the white rulers, and a handful of Europeans administered vast areas without opposition. The British tended to rule through local chiefs, so most Africans were ruled by other Africans.

Agriculture was the main occupation, with Africans producing, for example, cocoa, palm oil or timber for export and with white farmers in East Africa employing native labour to grow tobacco, sisal, cotton and coffee. In the Rhodesias and South Africa (which alone had a considerable white population) mining was leading to industrial development.

The attitude of the colonial powers was that there was no need for haste: the colonial system would last for centuries and it was the government's job to keep order and leave education to the

△ **Abd el Krim,** Moroccan chief who fought the Spanish and the French in the twenties, one of the few who actively opposed the Europeans.

missionaries, trade and economic advance to private enterprise.

Nevertheless, change was in the air. Germany's former colonies were now held as mandates until their people could "stand on their own feet". Lord Lugard and the Frenchman, Albert Saurrat, expressed the view that the Africans should be helped forward; government should be in the people's interests, while Africa's resources should be for the benefit of the world. In practice, it was difficult to make this ideal work.

There was an interesting difference in the attitudes of the British and of the other powers. In theory, Africans in French, Belgian and Portuguese colonies were to become citizens of those countries, able to attend their universities and sit in their home parliaments. The British had no such idea, holding that the Africans should develop in their own way under British rule.

What of the Africans themselves during this period? Independence was scarcely even a dream, for leaders were mostly concerned with tribal affairs and with squeezing out concessions from their rulers. They wanted education and civilization on European lines, not independence, so they adopted the Europeans' dress, education system and religion.

The mission schools provided basic education for young Africans, while a select few went on to colleges like Achimota in the Gold Coast and Makerere in Uganda. These were the seedbeds for Africa's future leaders, but for the moment, nationalism had hardly stirred.

◁ **African children** on their way to school: education made good progress, with Britain and Belgium aiding their mission schools, while the French set up state schools. Students usually went overseas to universities.

The Landlords
of Africa in 1925

Europe's domination of Africa after the First World War; France had the biggest empire, ruling nearly half the continent, though much of France's territory was sparsely inhabited. Great Britain came next and Belgium, Portugal and Italy all held large territories.

Britain's protectorate over Egypt was ended in 1922, and the only other independent countries were Ethiopia and Liberia. Germany's colonies had become mandates of the League of Nations, Britain receiving German East Africa with parts of Togoland and the Cameroons, while France took most of the latter two colonies. Belgium gained part of German East Africa and the Union of South Africa took over German West Africa.

The diagram top right shows comparative sizes of the areas under colonial rule, while populations are shown below, left.

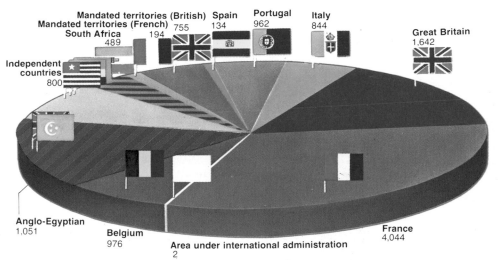

Mandated territories (British) — **Spain** 755 134
Mandated territories (French) — 194
South Africa 489
Portugal 962
Italy 844
Great Britain 1,642
Independent countries 800
Anglo-Egyptian 1,051
Belgium 976
Area under international administration 2
France 4,044

Figures in thousands of square miles

Independent countries
26,055

Great Britain and dominions
40,868

France
32,854

Belgium
18,000

Portugal
7,717

Anglo-Egyptian
5,825

Mandated territories (British and South African)
5,210

Mandated territories (French)
3,747

Italy
2,105

Spain
945

Area under international administration
75

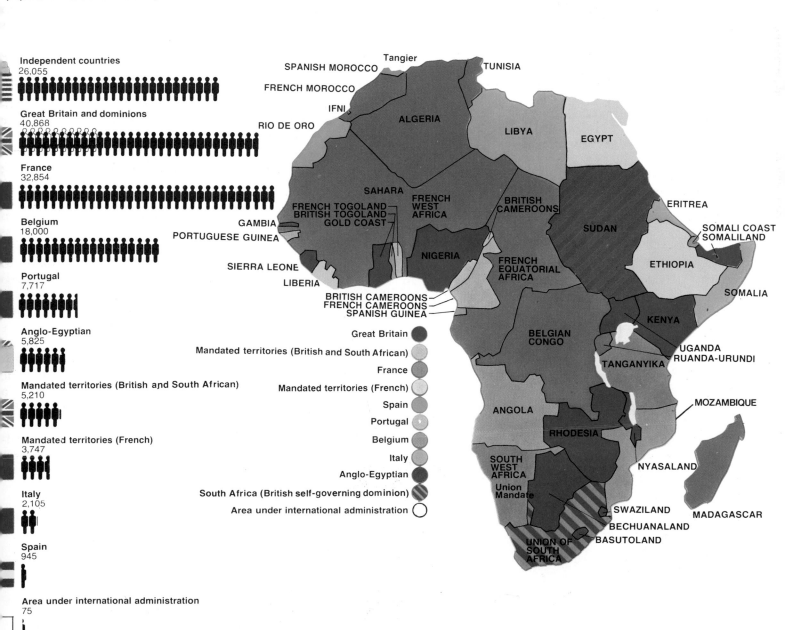

Great Britain
Mandated territories (British and South African)
France
Mandated territories (French)
Spain
Portugal
Belgium
Italy
Anglo-Egyptian
South Africa (British self-governing dominion)
Area under international administration

SPANISH MOROCCO
Tangier
TUNISIA
FRENCH MOROCCO
IFNI
ALGERIA
LIBYA
EGYPT
RIO DE ORO
SAHARA
FRENCH WEST AFRICA
BRITISH CAMEROONS
ERITREA
FRENCH TOGOLAND
BRITISH TOGOLAND
GOLD COAST
GAMBIA
PORTUGUESE GUINEA
SIERRA LEONE
LIBERIA
BRITISH CAMEROONS
FRENCH CAMEROONS
SPANISH GUINEA
NIGERIA
SUDAN
SOMALI COAST
SOMALILAND
ETHIOPIA
SOMALIA
FRENCH EQUATORIAL AFRICA
KENYA
BELGIAN CONGO
UGANDA
RUANDA-URUNDI
TANGANYIKA
ANGOLA
MOZAMBIQUE
RHODESIA
SOUTH WEST AFRICA
Union Mandate
NYASALAND
SWAZILAND
MADAGASCAR
BECHUANALAND
BASUTOLAND
UNION OF SOUTH AFRICA

Figures in thousands

47

The Wall Street Crash

△ **Jubilation on Wall Street,** home of the New York Stock Exchange, as prices keep rising.

The "Gay Twenties" ended on a disastrous note. The world seemed to be recovering from the effects of war; trade had picked up and production was rising, when the New York Stock Market suddenly collapsed, bringing the world's economy to ruins.

During the war, America had lent vast sums to the warring powers and in the early twenties she extended further loans to countries struggling to get back on their feet. Germany, in particular, received colossal sums and Europe became dangerously dependent upon American dollars.

Still, the American scene looked good. Business was booming and prices of shares bought and sold on the New York Stock Market went up and up. A man who bought shares in a company for 100 dollars could soon find them worth double, treble and even five times what he had paid.

Confident that they could not lose, people borrowed money in order to buy shares which on paper were worth a fortune. This was fine as long as prices went on rising until, one day in October 1929, someone big started to sell large amounts of shares; rumours went round, and suddenly everyone decided to sell their shares, too. Since there were few buyers, prices dropped like a stone and shares, recently so valuable, became almost worthless.

Borrowers went bankrupt; banks and businesses closed down and the reverberations of the crash spread across the world.

In America, when money dried up and factories closed because the once-rich had stopped buying consumer goods, workers became unemployed. Then they bought less and more businesses failed and yet more people were out of work. It was like some ghastly game of consequences.

In Europe and South America, the collapse of American prosperity brought economic troubles and disastrous unemployment. Governments tried to protect their failing home industries by putting tariffs on other countries' goods, but this hampered world trade and made the situation worse. There was a world glut of food which could not reach the hungry millions because prices fell too low to pay transport costs, so farmers burnt their crops and slaughtered the livestock they could not sell. The whole world fell into what was known as the Great Depression.

◁ **A prophetic German cartoon of 1927:** rich financiers, enjoying themselves regardless of the poor, are in fact on the brink of a crash. America's wealth was owned by too few of its citizens.

△ **New York, October 1929:** a victim of the crash tries desperate measures to raise cash. Like many others, he had probably bought shares with money he had borrowed.

△ **Herbert Hoover,** President of the United States, who was criticized for saying that the country's economy was basically sound. America *was* rich but its economic structure was shaky and when confidence departed, the crash followed.

△ **Effects of the crash in France:** unemployed queue for free soup. Britain soon had three million, and Germany six million, unemployed.

▷ **Diagram showing how the New York stock market rose and fell in the twenties:** the taller columns indicate the number of shares bought and sold, while the other column shows comparative prices.

1929 is the peak year; after that, prices and volume of business fall drastically and 1932 prices barely reach a quarter of the 1929 high. The Crash started on October 19 and, in the next ten days, the losses so shattered the nation's confidence that it took years for business and industry to recover.

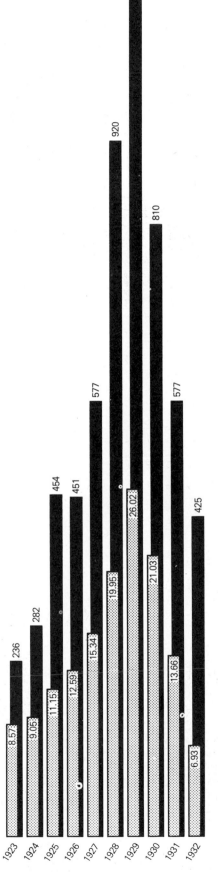

Developments on the Stock Exchange

■ Volume of Sales on New York Stock Exchange (millions of shares)

▨ Index of common stock prices (1941-43 = 10)

Year	Volume of Sales	Index of common stock prices
1923	236	8.57
1924	282	9.05
1925	454	11.15
1926	451	12.59
1927	577	15.34
1928	920	19.95
1929	1,125	26.02
1930	810	21.03
1931	577	13.66
1932	425	6.93

49

Literature in the Twenties

The changing pace of life and the violent contrasts which characterized the period can be seen in its literature. The literary "establishment" continued to flourish, but new kinds of writing emerged.

Reading was still the chief leisure activity of many people in the twenties, despite growing competition from the cinema and radio. Poets like T. S. Eliot, Yeats, Belloc, Chesterton and Ezra Pound appealed perhaps to a select few, but novelists were more popular, especially those writing in the traditional manner, that is, telling a story in which characters and plot provide the interest.

Galsworthy completed *The Forsyte Saga* (1925), Arnold Bennett wrote his Clayhanger novels and J. B. Priestley's *The Good Companions* had people queuing in the flourishing circulating libraries. Aldous Huxley was perhaps the most brilliant of the younger school, while Lytton Strachey startled people with acid-sharp biographies.

Meanwhile, Sinclair Lewis and Scott Fitzgerald were producing their disillusioned pictures of the American scene. There was brisk demand, too, for less literary works like those by Warwick Deeping and Munthe, and for the thrillers by Edgar Wallace and "Sapper".

The period was more remarkable for the number of "high-brow" writers who did not want to write in the traditional style. In their different ways, Proust, James Joyce, Kafka, Virginia Woolf, D. H. Lawrence and Gertrude Stein were literary rebels, more concerned with feelings than with story or action, and especially with the workings of the subconscious mind. Some, like Joyce and Lawrence, also wanted to free the novel from the restrictions imposed by polite society on coarse language and descriptions of sexual love.

The best of the war novels appeared some years after the Armistice, as though it took time before writers could bear to unburden themselves of the horrors of the war. Mottram's *Spanish Farm* appeared in 1924, Hemingway's *A Farewell to Arms* in 1925, while Aldington's *Death of a Hero* and Remarque's *All Quiet on the Western Front* came out in 1929.

△ **Ernest Hemingway,** the American novelist and **Sylvia Beach** outside her famous bookshop, Shakespeare and Co. in Paris, a meeting-place for English and American writers.

Hemingway, who lived in Paris from 1921 to 1926, had served with the Italian forces and had been wounded. He based his novel—*Farewell to Arms*—on his wartime experiences.

Hemingway's powerful style and staccato dialogue inspired a whole school of "tough" writers. In his own life, he resembled the characters he wrote about, adventurous, brutal and hard-drinking.

△ **Scott Fitzgerald and his wife, Zelda:** this American novelist was the typical figure of the jazz age, one of the "lost generation". In *The Beautiful and the Damned* (1922), he expressed the cynicism of his contemporaries In *The Great Gatsby* (1925), he described the tragic love affair of a shady financier in the days of jazz and bootleg liquor.

△ Two of the literary figures in Paris, **Ford Madox Ford,** the English writer, and **James Joyce.** Ford founded the *Transatlantic Review* in Paris to publish the work of expatriate writers.

Joyce, born in Dublin, lived most of his life abroad. He finally settled in Paris where Sylvia Beach published his novel *Ulysses,* a work of genius which was banned in most countries. It is a difficult novel to read, dense in thought and complex in structure, but it contains brilliant passages of description and characterization.

△ **Virginia Woolf** was the most gifted member of the "Bloomsbury Group", a number of writers and artists in London. She came to feel that the traditional novels of people like Wells, Galsworthy and Bennett, for all their concentration upon factual description, were unsatisfactory.

In *Mrs Dalloway* (1925), *To the Lighthouse* (1927) and *The Waves,* she explored the subconscious world of mood and sensation. Rejecting story, plot and to some extent character, she took the novel as near as possible to poetry.

△ **D. H. Lawrence,** English poet and novelist, who, like Joyce, Hemingway, Ezra Pound, Gertrude Stein and many other writers and artists, could not settle down in his own country. Lawrence travelled incessantly in Germany, Austria, America, Mexico and Sicily, searching in vain for health and contentment.

His best known novels include *Sons and Lovers, Women in Love* and *Lady Chatterley's Lover* (1928). Though opinions vary about the quality of his work, he had a tremendous influence on young writers who felt that he explored human emotions with a new honesty.

△ **T. E. Lawrence,** often called "Lawrence of Arabia", lived with the Arabs during World War One, won their confidence and led the tribesmen in a series of campaigns against the Turks.

He became deeply involved in the Arab cause and, feeling that the Peace Conference failed to grant what he had fought for and indeed promised, he changed his name and joined the Royal Air Force as Aircraftsman Shaw. He described the desert campaign in *The Seven Pillars of Wisdom* (1926) a superb work which is marvellously exciting and ultimately tragic. He also wrote *Revolt in the Desert* (1927).

△ **Sinclair Lewis,** the American best-selling novelist who saw with clear eyes the follies and weaknesses of his countrymen. In *Main Street* (1920), he satirizes the intolerance of small town life, while *Babitt* (1922) lays bare the smug materialism of the American businessman. Other novels in similar vein are *Martin Arrowsmith,* and *Elmer Gantry*.

△ **Marcel Proust,** who died in 1922, suffered from chronic ill-health. As a young man he moved in smart Parisian society, but on the death of his mother, he shut himself up in a sound-proof room to write his masterpiece in 13 volumes, the longest novel ever written, *A la Recherche du Temps Perdu.*

Proust delved into every detail of his childhood and beneath the surface of ordinary life to discover the innermost experiences of human beings.

The Main Events 1919-1929

1919

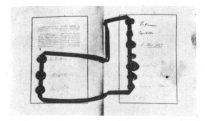

The signatures on the Treaty of Versailles.

January: Peace Conference opens in Paris, dominated by the "Big Three", Clemenceau, Wilson, Lloyd George.
March: Soviet Russia, Comintern, organization of world Communist parties, formed.
April: India, 379 civilians killed at Amritsar.
May: Turkey, Kemal organizes resistance to Greeks.
June: Treaty of Versailles signed with Germany. German Fleet scuttled at Scapa Flow.
August: Rumanians invade Hungary to overthrow Bela Kun's Communist régime. Germany, Weimar Constitution adopted.
September: Treaty of St Germain signed with Austria. Italian patriot, d'Annunzio, seizes port of Fiume.
December: Government of India Act gives Indians greater share in provincial affairs. Government of Ireland Act gives North and South their own parliaments.
General: Women over 20 get vote in Germany. Lady Astor first woman M.P. in Britain. Prohibition introduced in Norway. Rutherford splits the nucleus. Alcock and Brown fly the Atlantic.
Cinema: *The Cabinet of Dr. Caligari,* German surrealist film.
Design: Gropius founds the Bauhaus in Weimar, a school of design for architects, painters, sculptors.
Music: *The Miraculous Mandarin* by Bartok. *The Three-cornered Hat* by de Falla.
Painting: Renoir, the French artist, dies.
Theatre: G. B. Shaw's play *Heartbreak House.*

1920

Royal Irish Constabulary: war in Ireland.

January: Prohibition introduced in America.
March: Right-wing Kapp Putsch defeated in Berlin. Counter-revolutionary Admiral Horthy becomes Regent in Hungary. U.S. Senate refuses to ratify Treaty of Versailles.
April: India, Gandhi launches civil disobedience campaign. Irish Volunteers (I.R.A.) attack police barracks.
May: Polish army invades Ukraine.
June: Turkey, Kemal fights Greeks in Asia Minor.
November: Warren Harding elected President of U.S. First Assembly of League of Nations. Final defeat of Whites in Russia.
December: Government of Ireland Bill passed, setting up two parliaments in Ireland.
General: Black and Tans recruited to fight Irish nationalists. Women given the federal vote in U.S.A. Unemployment benefit introduced for most British workers. Dame Nellie Melba broadcasts from Chelmsford in Britain. Public broadcasting begins in America.
Cinema: Charlie Chaplin in *The Kid,* Mary Pickford and Douglas Fairbanks screen-idols. Flaherty's documentary, *Nanook of the North.*
Literature: Sinclair Lewis, *Main Street,* Wilfred Owen's *Poems* published posthumously.
Music: Cocteau and Les Six in Paris. Paul Whiteman's Jazz Band visits Europe.
Painting: Dada "anti-art" exhibition in Cologne. Modigliani dies in Paris.

1921

Charlie Chaplin, genius of the silent screen.

March: Soviet Russia, Lenin launches his New Economic Policy. Anglo-Russian trade treaty. Trotsky crushes Krondstadt Rising against Bolsheviks.
April: Miners on strike in Britain; on "Black Friday", other unions refuse to support them. President Harding announces U.S. will take no part in League of Nations.
June: First Northern Ireland parliament meets in Belfast. King George makes plea for peace.
July: Communist Party founded in China. Abd el Krim defeats Spanish army in Morocco.
December: Agreement between Britain and the Irish nationalists sets up Irish Free State.
General: Disorders and Hindu-Moslem enmity in India. Paris Reparation Commission orders Germany to pay £6,650m. Inflation in Germany. Unemployment exceeds one million. Car production booming in U.S.
Cinema: Meteoric rise of Rudolph Valentino.
Literature: D. H. Lawrence, *Women in Love;* Aldous Huxley, *Crome Yellow;* Lytton Strachey, *Queen Victoria.*
Painting: Picasso, *Three Musicians*
Theatre: Pirandello, *Six Characters in Search of an Author.*

1922

The March on Rome.

February: Treaty of Washington; Britain, U.S., Japan agree to limit capital ships in proportion 5:5:3.
March: Egypt becomes independent under King Fuad.
April: Treaty of Rapallo between Germany and Russia establishes friendly relations to dismay of France and Britain.
August: Turks defeat Greeks at Smyrna, Asia Minor.
September: Chanak crisis, Turks confront British troops. Palestine, British Mandate proclaimed.
October: In Britain, Conservatives withdraw support from Lloyd George, who resigns. Bonar Law Prime Minister. In Turkey, Kemal proclaims Republic, abolishing the sultanate. In Italy, Mussolini's "March on Rome"; Fascists in power.
December: Union of Soviet Socialist Republics (U.S.S.R.) formed.
Ireland: Dominion Status rejected by Sinn Fein; civil war; assassination of Michael Collins, Irish leader.
General: Prohibition in U.S. leads to bootlegging and crime. Ill-feeling between France and Germany over reparations. Broadcasting services begin in London. British Broadcasting Company formed. Insulin treatment introduced for diabetes.
Literature: James Joyce, *Ulysses;* Sinclair Lewis, *Babbitt.* T. S. Eliot, *The Waste Land.*
Painting: Klee at work in Germany.

1923

Adolf Hitler in 1923.

January: Ruhr occupied by French troops.
April: Ceasefire concluded in Ireland.
May: In Britain, Stanley Baldwin succeeds Bonar Law as Prime Minister.
July: Treaty of Lausanne settles Turkey's frontiers.
August: In U.S., Harding dies, Coolidge becomes President. In Germany, Stresemann becomes Chancellor.
September: In Spain, de Rivera becomes dictator.
October: Kemal becomes President of Turkish Republic.
November: In Germany, Hitler's Munich Putsch fails.
General: Strikes and unemployment rife in Europe and U.S. Germans adopt passive resistance in Ruhr. Colossal inflation in Germany. Reparations Commission states Germany deliberately defaulting on debts. In Britain, first football Cup Final at Wembley. In Italy, Mussolini consolidates his dictatorial powers. In U.S. *Time* magazine first published. Tetanus and diptheria injections introduced.
Cinema: Erich von Stroheim's *Greed.*
Literature: Aldous Huxley *Antic Hay,* Hilaire Belloc *Sonnets and Verse.*
Music: Kodaly and Honegger.
Theatre: G. B. Shaw, *Saint Joan.* Death of French actress, Sarah Bernhardt.

1924

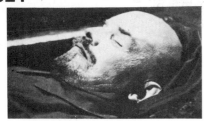

Lenin, founder of Communist Russia.

January: In U.S.S.R., Lenin dies without nominating successor. In Britain, first Labour Government; Ramsay Macdonald becomes Prime Minister.
March: Greece becomes a Republic. Hitler tried and sent to prison.
April: Dawes plan introduced to help economic recovery of Germany and to fix reparations.
June: In Italy, murder of socialist leader Matteotti.
October: In Britain, General Election; Zinoviev letter scare, whereby Communist Party was supposed to be instructed to take over the Labour movement. Baldwin Prime Minister again. Anglo-German trade treaty. In Italy, non-Fascist trade unions dissolved.
General: Situation less tense with German

co-operation in Ruhr. Two U.S. Douglas biplanes fly round the world in 15 days. Alan Cobham surveys air route to India. Ten million Model "T" Fords on U.S. roads. Fascist strong-arm methods in Italy. Appleton discovers Heaviside and Appleton atmospheric layers. Tuberculosis vaccine introduced.
Cinema: Douglas Fairbanks, *The Thief of Bagdad.*
Literature: E. M. Forster, *A Passage to India*; Thomas Mann, *The Magic Mountain.* Deaths of Kafka and Conrad.
Music: Gershwin, *Rhapsody in Blue.*
Painting: Surrealism.
Theatre: Sean O'Casey, *Juno and the Paycock.*

1925

Emancipation of women in Germany.

January: U.S.S.R., Trotsky dismissed as war minister.
March: In China, Sun Yat-sen dies and is eventually succeeded as Nationalist leader by Chiang Kai-shek.
April: In Germany, Hindenburg elected President. Britain returns to the gold standard at pre-1914 rate. This reduces burden of American debt but makes it harder to sell British exports.
July: Scopes trial in U.S.
October: Locarno Pact guaranteeing Franco-German, Belgian-German frontiers, leads to era of apparent goodwill in Europe.
November: Coolidge elected President of U.S. In Italy, Mussolini tightens press control, arrests opponents. French troops withdraw from Ruhr.

League of Nations prestige high with improvement in international relations. In Britain, old age pensions granted to persons over 65. Some economic recovery and trade improvement. Alan Cobham flies to South Africa. In U.S., Al Capone in command of Chicago underworld. In Turkey, Kemal introduces laws to westernize the country.
Architecture: Bauhaus buildings at Dessau.
Cinema: Chaplin, *The Gold Rush*; Eisenstein, *Battleship Potemkin.*
Literature: Kafka's *The Trial* published posthumously; Scott Fitzgerald, *The Great Gatsby.*
Music: Shostakovich, First Symphony. Berg *Wozzeck.*
Painting: Picasso's *Three Dancers.*

1926

Cobham returns from his 26,000 mile trip.

May: In Britain, General Strike lasts nine days and ends in defeat for the unions. Miners stay out on strike. In Ireland, De Valera forms Fianna Fail party. Pilsudski's military coup overthrows government in Poland. Abd-El-Krim defeated by Franco-Spanish forces in Morocco.
June: Chiang Kai-shek attacks northern warlords.
July: Financial crisis in France and Belgium.
September: Germany joins the League of Nations.
October: In U.S.S.R., Stalin defeats opponents and expels Trotsky from Politburo. Alan Cobham completes flight from Britain to Australia and back.
November: Coal-miners return to work in Britain. Imperial conference declare British Dominions

autonomous and equal, "freely associated as members of the British Commonwealth".
General: Anglo-Egyptian Treaty, British forces withdraw to Canal Zone. Army coup overthrows republican government in Portugal. J. L. Baird demonstrates television in London. Richard Byrd makes first aeroplane flight to North Pole.
Cinema: Death of Rudolph Valentino. Greta Garbo's film debut. Fritz Lang, *Metropolis.*
Literature: T. E. Lawrence, *Seven Pillars of Wisdom.* Kafka *The Castle.* Edna Ferber, *Show Boat.*
Music: Puccini, *Turandot*; Jelly Roll Morton, jazz.
Painting: Klee, Picasso. Braque.
Sculpture: Epstein *The Visitation.*

1927

Chiang Kai-shek, China's Nationalist leader.

April: In China, Chiang Kai-shek organizes Kuomintang government at Nanking: makes all-out attack on Communists.
May: In Britain, Trades Disputes Act makes certain strikes illegal and hampers trade union activities. Lindbergh makes non-stop New York–Paris flight. In Australia, Parliament House opened at Canberra.
July: Violent enmity between government and de Valera's Republicans in Irish Free State. Socialist riots and general strike in Vienna.
August: Mao Tse-tung founds Red Army of China. De Valera agrees to take oath and seat in Dail.
September: President Hindenburg repudiates German responsibility for the war.

December: Stalin secures banishment of Trotsky in U.S.S.R. In India, Simon Commission investigates situation; is boycotted by most Indian parties. Lemaitre puts forward "big bang" theory of origin of the universe. Segrave exceeds 200 m.p.h. on land. Britain wins Schneider Trophy air race, at 281 m.p.h.
Architecture: Le Corbusier in France.
Cinema: Al Jolson, *The Jazz Singer,* first talkie.
Literature: Thorton Wilder, *The Bridge of San Luis Rey.* Henry Williamson, *Tarka the Otter.* Virginia Woolf, *To the Lighthouse.*
Music: Shostakovich, Prokofief, Stravinsky, Jerome Kern.

1928

Mickey Mouse in his first cartoon film.

April: Chiang Kai-shek captures Peking; makes Nanking capital of China; Japanese troops occupy Shantung. Salazar becomes minister of finance and leading political figure in Portugal.
May: In Italy, universal suffrage abolished.
June: Franc devalued in France. Kingsford Smith flies Pacific from California to Brisbane, Australia.
July: Britain, "flapper" vote for women over 21.
August: Kellogg-Briand Pact signed by most nations, renouncing war—the high-water mark for the League of Nations. Independence of India League calls for complete independence.
October: U.S.S.R., first Five Year Plan for industry.

November: U.S., Herbert Hoover elected President.
December: Britain makes treaty with China. Gandhi demands Dominion status for India within one year.
General: strikes, especially in Bombay. Alexander Fleming discovers penicillin.
Cinema: Disney, first Mickey Mouse cartoon.
Music: Bartok, String Quartet No 4; Ravel, *Bolero*; Gershwin; Schoenberg; Louis Armstrong.
Painting: Braque, Utrillo.
Theatre: Brecht, *Threepenny Opera.*

1929

Al Capone, Chicago gangster.

January: In Yugoslavia, King Alexander proclaims dictatorship.
February: In Italy, Lateran Treaties make peace between state and the Roman Catholic Church. U.S., St. Valentine's Day massacre; Capone now at height of his power.
March: Italy, election of an all-Fascist parliament.
May: Britain, Labour victory in General Election.
June: Young Plan for final settlement of German reparations by 1988.
July: France, Poincaré resigns premiership.
August: Palestine, Arab attacks on Jews, riots.
October: Britain resumes relations with Russia.
America: Wall Street Crash, loans to Europe ended. India promised Dominion status.

General: In Britain, first woman Cabinet Minister, Margaret Bondfield. Hunger march by Glasgow unemployed. B.B.C. begins experimental television programmes. In South Africa, term "apartheid" first used to mean separate development. In France, commencement of Maginot Line fortifications. In U.S.S.R., Stalin now dictator of Russia. U.S., Admiral Byrd flies over South Pole. Airship *Graf Zeppelin* flies round the world.
Literature: Hemingway, *A Farewell to Arms*; Priestley, *The Good Companions;* Aldington, *Death of a Hero.*
Theatre: Sheriff, *Journey's End.*
Painting: Augustus John, Paul Nash.
Sculpture: Henry Moore, *Reclining Figure.*

Who Was Who in the Twenties

△ Aristide Briand and Primo de Rivera

Baird, John Logie (1888-1946), studied electrical engineering at Glasgow University and tried his hand at various business enterprises before ill-health forced him to retire in 1922 to Hastings. Here, he began experiments to transmit pictures by radio. By 1924, he managed to transmit the silhouette of a Maltese cross a distance of three yards. He moved to London where he became practically destitute until rescued by his family. Success in transmitting a picture of a boy's face led to a public demonstration of television and, in 1928, he transmitted pictures of people in London to a receiver in New York.

Baldwin, Stanley (1867-1947) made a fortune in the family iron and steel business before entering politics at the age of 39. In 1922, he played a leading role in bringing about the downfall of Lloyd George and, in the following year, as Chancellor of the Exchequer, he agreed to pay British debts to America irrespective of whether Britain's debtors paid up. This quixotic agreement brought him a certain prestige, but it was nevertheless a surprise when he succeeded Bonar Law as Prime Minister in 1923.

Beneath an indolent manner, Baldwin was shrewd and tough; he out-manoeuvred the union leaders in the General Strike and appealed to many people as the plain honest man of politics. However, his failure to tackle unemployment vigorously lost him the 1929 election to Ramsey Macdonald.

Briand, Aristide (1862-1932) was French premier no less than eleven times during his career, but his greatest achievements were in foreign affairs. His friendship with Stresemann did much to establish cordial Franco-German relations in the late twenties.

Chiang Kai-shek (1887-1975) joined Dr Sun Yat-sen's revolutionary party while a student at a Japanese military academy. He went to Russia for a time and returned to China to train Kuomintang officers on Russian lines. When Sun died in 1925, Chiang became commander-in-chief of the Kuomintang forces and, with Communist help, defeated some of the warlords. In 1927, he carried out a bloodthirsty purge of the Communists who went underground to organize resistance. As President of the Chinese Republic, Chiang achieved an uneasy unification of the country.

Coolidge, Calvin (1872-1933), was President of the United States for much of the twenties. While America was enjoying unexampled prosperity (and the fruits of Prohibition) Coolidge was inclined to let things drift along and he failed to warn the country of the dangers of Stock Exchange gambling.

Eisenstein, Sergei Mikhailovich (1898-1948), the great Russian film director, was born the son of a shipbuilder. He was trained as a civil engineer, and built trenches for the Bolsheviks during the Russian Revolution.

After gaining some experience in the theatre, Eisenstein went on to make films, and in 1924 he directed *Potemkin,* the story of a mutiny on a battleship in Tsarist Russia. The film won international acclaim for its realism, and highly advanced technique.

Gandhi, Mohandas Karamchand (1869-1948), studied law in London and spent 21 years in the Indian community of South Africa, before returning to India to become the dominant personality of Congress. His civil disobedience campaign of 1920 led to violent disorders and Gandhi was in prison from 1922-1924. After a period of retirement, he returned to politics in 1927 and was elected President of Congress, though he declined the office.

By this time, he was India's national leader, a saintly emaciated figure, revered by millions for his moral teachings, courage and personal example of adopting the poverty of most of his countrymen.

There were puzzling contradictions in his nature; on the one hand, he advocated a return to simple rural life, on the other, he accepted the support of Indian big business; he observed the purest forms of Hindu religion but offended orthodox Hindus by championing the "untouchables".

△ George Gershwin

Gershwin, George (1898-1937), was born in New York where he studied music in the traditional way and had to earn a living by playing the piano in a jazz shop. During the twenties, he composed a number of Broadway musical comedies, including *Our Nell, Lady Be Good* and *Tell Me More.* For Paul Whiteman, the band leader, he wrote his famous *Rhapsody in Blue* which was followed by *Concerto in F* and *An American in Paris.* Gershwin brought great skill and originality to symphonic jazz and also to popular songs and musical comedy.

Hindenburg, Paul Ludwig (1847-1934) was the Prussian general who, with Ludendorff, commanded Germany's land forces during World War One and organized the retreat of the beaten armies. As a national hero, he was elected President of the German Republic in 1925, a dignified figure who resolutely denied Germany's responsibility for the war. Though he did not oppose Stresemann's enlightened politics, he failed to realise the evil nature of Nazism.

Hitler, Adolf (1889-1945). In 1920, the failed artist, former housepainter and corporal was living in Munich where he joined an insignificant political party which he re-named the National Socialist German Workers' Party, afterwards known as the Nazis. Through his raving attacks on Jews and Marxists, he attracted a following of uniformed thugs and, in 1923, believing that the Weimar Republic was about to collapse, Hitler, with Ludendorff, Roehm and Goering attempted to seize power.

The Munich Putsch was a fiasco and Hitler was arrested and sentenced to five years' imprisonment. But the Putsch had made him well-known and, in prison, he wrote *Mein Kampf,* setting down his beliefs and how he intended to carry them out. Released after only one year, he set about rebuilding the Nazi party and by 1929 had become its undisputed leader.

△ Mustapha Kemal

Kafka, Franz (1883-1924), the German–Jewish novelist published little during his lifetime. He was uncertain of the literary value of his work, and left instructions that his manuscripts should be destroyed after his death.

It is lucky that his instructions were not obeyed; his three most famous works, *The Trial, The Castle* and *Amerika* would have been lost. Kafka's novels show man in a strange and threatening universe, and reveal a disturbing, profoundly original genius.

Kemal, Mustafa (1880-1938), also known as Ataturk, commanded Turkish forces during the war. After his country's defeat, he organized the nationalist army which finally defeated the Greeks at Smyrna in 1922 and cleared them out of Asia Minor. Kemal then overthrew the Sultan and was elected President of the Turkish Republic in 1923.

He devoted himself to transforming his backward country into a modern state, introducing Western education, justice, dress, and votes for women. Though many of his reforms clashed with Muslim beliefs, he met with surprisingly little opposition and was revered as the founder of modern Turkey.

Lenin, Vladimir (1870-1924), after years of revolutionary activity in exile, Lenin returned to Russia in 1917 to overthrow the Provincial Government and, with ruthless single-mindedness, to establish the Bolsheviks in power. For three years, he grappled with civil war but, by the end of 1921, he was master of Russia, faced with the task of rebuilding the devastated country.

To get industry and agriculture back on its feet, he introduced his New Economic Policy, allowing a certain amount of private enterprise, as a temporary breathing-space before the country was ready for all-out Communism. So great was his hold on the Party, that there was no question of replacing him until his death in 1924.

Lindbergh, Charles (1902-1974), although pilots like Cobham, Byrd and Kingsford-Smith could claim greater experience and more varied feats of long-distance flying, Lindbergh became the most celebrated aviator of the decade, through making the first non-stop solo flight across the Atlantic. In his Ryan monoplane, *The Spirit of St Louis,* he took off from New York on May 20, 1927 and landed at Le Bourget, Paris, 33 hours later.

Lloyd George, David (1863-1945), was known as the "Welsh Wizard". One of the Big Three, with Clemenceau and Woodrow Wilson, he was a major force at the Peace Conference and, during the next three years, he was incessantly engaged with Ireland's struggle and with international conferences settling the affairs of Europe.

Yet, in Britain, his position became increasingly shaky. A Liberal, he presided over a coalition government dominated by Conservatives who had never liked or trusted him. Moreover, he seemed too busy to give his mind to the problem of unemployment and falling trade. When, in October 1922, the Conservatives withdrew from the coalition, Lloyd George was forced to resign. He never held office again.

△ Poincaré and Lloyd George

Macdonald, James Ramsey (1866-1937). Brought up in poverty in Scotland, Macdonald became prominent in the infant Labour party of pre-war years. He lost influence by opposing the war but, in 1922, he had regained the leadership and, when Liberal and Labour won the 1923 Election, he became Britain's first Labour Prime Minister. Though lacking an overall majority, he did remarkably well, especially in foreign affairs where he persuaded the French to accept the Dawes Plan for German Reparations. After less than a year, his government fell because the Liberals disliked his supposed leaning towards Communist Russia. Macdonald then led the Opposition until 1929, when he became premier for the second time.

Mussolini, Benito (1883-1945) is seen below with his nose bandaged after an Irishwoman had tried to assassinate him in 1926. By this time, the ex-newspaper editor was firmly established as dictator of Italy. After the war, he had formed the Fascist party to combat Communism and recruited black-shirt gangs to take virtual control of the northern cities.

In October 1922, he threatened to march on Rome whereupon King Victor Emmanuel invited him to form a new government.

In the twenties many people were impressed by the apparent efficiency of the Fascist regime; the country seemed better organized, business improved and a vast programme of public works helped to solve unemployment. Mussolini had a taste for pageantry and for striking poses; he organized enormous, self-glorifying rallies, and he also kept a private zoo, where he was in the habit of posing for the press with his pet lioness.

△ Benito Mussolini

Pilsudski, Joseph (1863-1935), before the war the Polish patriot worked to liberate his country from Russian rule and when war came, he formed a Polish legion to fight on the German side. However, he fell out with the Germans who interned him in 1916. Released at the armistice, he became President of Poland in 1919 with the rank of marshal, and in 1920 he led an army against the Bolsheviks. He captured Kiev but was driven back to Warsaw and when peace was made with Russia, he lost favour and retired.

In 1926, he overthrew the government by a military coup d'état and became Prime Minister with powers which became increasingly those of a dictator.

Poincaré, Raymond (1860-1934), served France as President throughout the war, and as premier from 1911-13, 1922-24 and 1926-29. Like most Frenchmen, he distrusted Germany and bitterly resented what he felt were German attempts to evade paying reparations. When Germany declared she could no longer pay, he sent French troops to occupy the Ruhr in 1923. He resigned in 1924 but came back two years later to solve a crisis of the French economy.

de Rivera, Primo (1870-1930), organized a military revolt in Spain in 1923. With King Alfonso's approval, he overthrew the constitution and set up a Fascist-type régime which lasted throughout the twenties. As dictator, he depended upon the Army and when, in 1929, he offended it by appointing some civilians to government posts, he was obliged to resign.

Rutherford, Ernest (1871-1937), the New Zealand-born physicist was working in England throughout the twenties, as Cavendish Professor of Experimental Physics at Cambridge. Already renowned for his scientific discoveries, he carried on research into nuclear physics which led eventually to the development of atomic power.

△ Antonio Salazar

Salazar, Antonio (1889-1970), who was to become another of Europe's dictators, came into prominence in 1928 when, as minister of finance, he re-organized Portugal's chaotic economic affairs. His success paved the way for his subsequent take-over of complete power.

Stresemann, Gustav (1878-1929), founded the German People's Party after the war and in 1923 was made Chancellor and foreign minister of the Weimar Republic. As foreign minister, he showed great skill in presenting Germany to the world as a reformed, peace-loving country. He negotiated the Locarno Pact with Britain and France and it was largely through his efforts that Germany was admitted to the League of Nations. He won the Nobel Peace Prize in 1926, but it is now believed that he was more of a nationalist than he revealed at the time and he approved the steps that were being taken to rebuild Germany's military strength.

Sun Yat-sen, (1886-1925), led the 1911 Revolution which overthrew the Manchu dynasty, and for a time was President of the new republic. General Yuan forced him into exile but, in 1923, he was back as President of the Southern Chinese Republic, reorganizing the Kuomintang with Russian help.

Looked on as the father of modern China, Sun Yat-sen was a social reformer who, while accepting Russian help, was never a convinced Communist.

Valentino, Rudolph (1895-1926), the heart-throb of the period was born in Italy and went to the United States in 1913. He was given his first major film role in 1921, and became a star overnight. Thousands attended his funeral five years later.

Wilson, Woodrow (1856-1924), as President of the United States, Wilson took America into the war in 1917 and, after it ended, played a leading part at the Peace Conference and in drawing up the Covenant of the League of Nations. Unfortunately, Americans did not share his enthusiasm for the League and in the Election of 1920, Wilson was overwhelmingly defeated by the Republican, Harding.

Model Cars

This project tells you how to make a collection of cars of the twenties in the form of silhouette-type scale models. The models can be mounted on a stand for display, or embedded in clear plastic.

Guide to scale sizes and grid card sizes

1/48th scale requires a grid size of $\frac{1}{4}$ in. squares. A suitable size for grid cards is 4 in. by 2 in.

1/64th scale requires a grid size of $\frac{3}{16}$ in. squares. A suitable size for grid cards is 3 in. by 2 in.

1/96th scale requires a grid size of $\frac{1}{8}$ in. squares. A suitable size for grid cards is 2 in. by $1\frac{1}{4}$ in.

Each square then represents 1 ft. (any scale).

Fig. 1

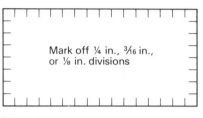

Mark off ¼ in., ³⁄₁₆ in., or ⅛ in. divisions

Fig. 2   Card cut to size

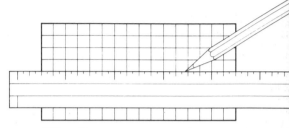

Fig. 3   Draw grid with ruler and pencil

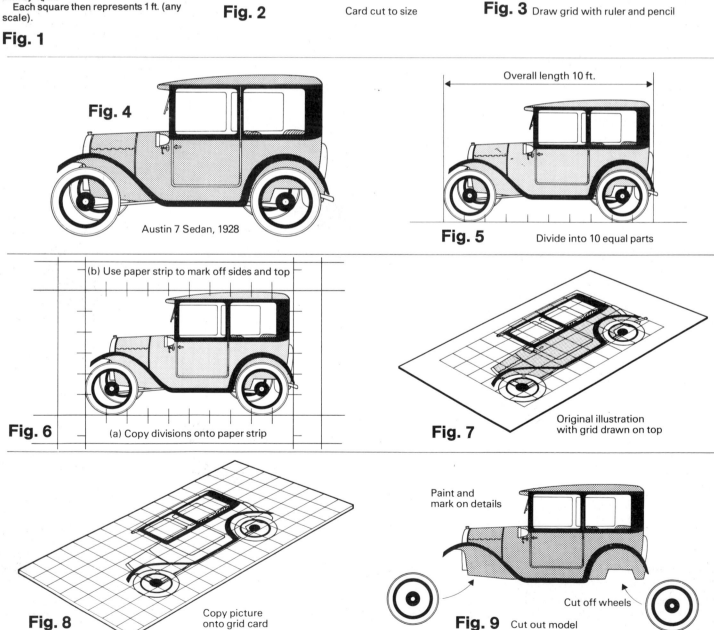

Fig. 4

Austin 7 Sedan, 1928

Overall length 10 ft.

Fig. 5   Divide into 10 equal parts

(b) Use paper strip to mark off sides and top

Fig. 6   (a) Copy divisions onto paper strip

Fig. 7   Original illustration with grid drawn on top

Fig. 8   Copy picture onto grid card

Paint and mark on details

Cut off wheels

Fig. 9   Cut out model

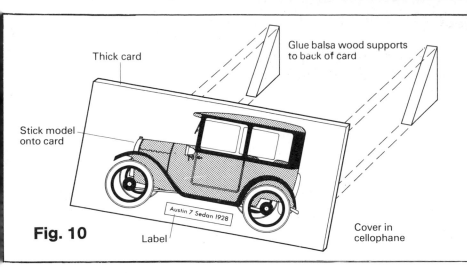

Mounting the model

The model can now be mounted on a piece of thick, stiff card, the same size as the original grid card. Glue the model in position, and add a typed label, showing the name of the car (Fig. 10).

To make the mounted model stand up, cut two pieces of balsa, as shown, and stick to the back of the card. The space between the supports can be filled with a "data panel" noting all the technical details you can find about the car.

To protect the model, cover the front with a piece of clear cellophane, cut slightly larger than the card, and folded over the edges. Glue the edges down or secure them with cellulose tape.

Fig. 10

Thick card

Glue balsa wood supports to back of card

Stick model onto card

Label

Cover in cellophane

Austin 7 Sedan 1928

First decide on your scale
All the models should be to the same scale. Since the idea is to build up a collection, each model should not be too large, so choose a scale from the following: 1/48th, 1/64th or 1/96th (see Fig. 1).

If all your models are to be mounted to stand up, like a small picture, then the largest scale (1/48th) will be best. If you want to mount each model in a plastic casting, then the smallest scale (1/96th) should be chosen.

If you think that a mixed collection of mounted and cast models would be a better choice, choose the 1/64th scale.

Prepare your grid cards
Having decided on the scale you are going to use, the next step is to draw up a grid card. This is a piece of white card cut to the size required (see Fig. 1), on which is drawn a series of squares in pencil to form a grid.

To do this, mark off the correct scale divisions around the edge of the outline (Fig. 2) and then draw in the grid with a ruler and pencil (Fig. 3).

You will need one grid card for each model.

Choose a subject
Suppose you are going to make a model of a 1928 Austin 7 Sedan. All you need is a good colour photo or drawing, showing an Austin 7 Sedan in side view (Fig. 4).

Draw on a grid
The next step is a little more tricky. You need to know the approximate length of the full-size car, so that you can work out the scale. Draw a line on the illustration representing the ground and mark off on this line what you estimate to be the length of the car, to the nearest whole number of feet. Then divide this length equally into that number of feet (Fig. 5). For example, if your nearest whole number length is marked at 10 ft., divide this length into ten equal parts. If the outline of the car extends beyond this, add another 1 ft. division.

Then draw in a rectangle fully enclosing the outline of the car. Take a strip of paper and copy the 1 ft. markings on to it. Use this strip to mark 1 ft. divisions on the top and two sides of the rectangle (Fig. 6).

Finally join these marks to complete the grid over the illustration (Fig. 7).

Copy onto a grid card
The squares on your grid card represent 1 ft. So do the squares drawn over the illustration. You can now copy in pencil the outline of the illustration onto your grid card, using the lines of the grid as a guide (Fig. 8). Complete the grid card by drawing on window shapes and other important details.

Finish in colour
The pencil drawing on the grid card can now be finished in colour. In the case of saloon cars, windows can be left unpainted, or given a light colour wash, or painted black. At this stage, leave a blank area where the wheels are to go.

Completing the model
The painted drawing can now be cut out (Fig. 9). You can then mark on further details, like door handles, panel lines, etc.

The wheels are made separately. Draw circles of the correct size onto spare card, mark out and paint on the wheel details, and paint the tyres black. When they are dry, cut the wheels very carefully and glue them to the car.

Making a plastic casting

For this you need a plastic-casting kit, or a quantity of polyester casting resin and hardener. You can obtain either from most do-it-yourself or hobby shops. The finished casting can be single-sided (Fig. 13) or double-sided (Fig. 15). For a single-sided casting, finish the model as described above, but do not add the balsa supports. Take a piece of stiff acetate sheet, the same size as the card on which the model is mounted, but with about $\frac{1}{2}$ in. extra along each side. Cut the acetate sheet as shown in Fig. 11 and score it so that the outer tabs can be bent up to form a shallow tray around the car (Fig. 12). Use cellulose tape to secure the corners of the tray.

Follow the instructions supplied with the casting resin for mixing, making up only enough resin to half fill the tray.

Allow it to set for an hour or so, then make a second batch of resin and fill the tray. When the casting is quite hard and cool, remove the acetate (Fig. 13 shows the completed casting).

Special note: casting resins get quite hot when setting, which is why the whole casting is not poured in at one go.

For a double-sided casting, the technique is similar, but this time the model is not mounted on card. It must have paint and wheels on *both* sides.

Make one side of the plastic casting exactly as before. When finished, turn the casting over in order to prepare the other side of the model. Cut a strip of fairly stiff acetate sheet whose width is twice the depth of the casting you have just made.

Put this strip around the edge of the casting, as shown in Fig. 14, securing the joins with tape. Pour in the resin mix to complete the second half of the casting. Peel off the acetate strip when the plastic is set. Your model is then ready for display, embedded in a block of clear plastic (Fig. 15).

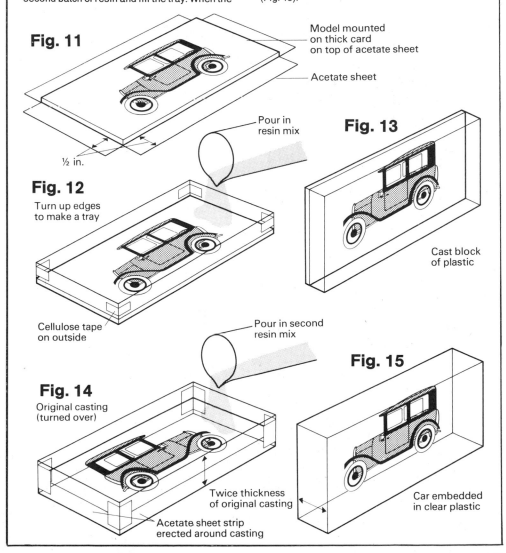

Fig. 11

Model mounted on thick card on top of acetate sheet

Acetate sheet

½ in.

Fig. 12

Turn up edges to make a tray

Cellulose tape on outside

Pour in resin mix

Fig. 13

Cast block of plastic

Fig. 14

Original casting (turned over)

Pour in second resin mix

Fig. 15

Car embedded in clear plastic

Twice thickness of original casting

Acetate sheet strip erected around casting

Record Charts

The twenties were wonderful years for progress in the design and performance of aircraft and cars – with records regularly being broken. This project tells you how to plot your own pictorial chart of individual records for pre-1920 to 1929.

Absolute Speed Records

Prior to 1920, Barney Oldfield driving a Benz car reached 131.72 m.p.h. (1910), although this was exceeded unofficially by aircraft during World War One.

Year		Speed	Country
1921	Lecointe (Nieuport-Delage)	210.64 m.p.h.	France
1922	Lecointe (Nieuport-Delage)	211.91 m.p.h.	France
	Mitchell (Curtiss R-6)	243.94 m.p.h.	U.S.
1923	Brown (Curtiss D-12)	274.20 m.p.h.	U.S.
1924	Bonnet (Bernard-Ferbois V-2)	278.47 m.p.h.	France
1927	Webster (Supermarine S5)	284.00 m.p.h.	Britain
	Webster (Supermarine S5) unofficial	300.00 m.p.h.	Britain
	Bernardi (Macchi M-52)	322.60 m.p.h.	Italy
	Williams (Kirk-Williams)	322.60 m.p.h.	U.S.
1928	Bernardi (Macchi M-52R)	348.60 m.p.h.	Italy
1929	Motta (Macchi 67)	362.00 m.p.h.	Italy
	Waghorn (Supermarine S6)	370.00 m.p.h.	Britain

Land Speed Records

Year		Speed	Country
1910	Barney Oldfield (Benz)	131.72 m.p.h.	U.S.
1922	Kenelm Lee Guiness (Sunbeam)	133.75 m.p.h.	Britain
1924	René Thomas (Delage)	143.31 m.p.h.	France
	Ernest Eldridge (Fiat)	146.01 m.p.h.	Italy
	Malcolm Campbell (Sunbeam)	146.16 m.p.h.	Britain
1926	J. G. Parry Thomas (Thomas)	171.02 m.p.h.	Britain
1927	Henry Segrave (Sunbeam)	203.79 m.p.h.	Britain
1928	Ray Keech (White Triplex)	207.55 m.p.h.	U.S.
1929	Henry Segrave (Golden Arrow)	231.44 m.p.h.	Britain

Above is a list of speed records broken in the twenties. Prior to World War One land vehicles (cars and trains) were faster than aeroplanes, but the wartime development of aircraft design and bigger, more powerful engines changed everything. Every absolute speed record from 1920 onwards was established by an aircraft. The first official record set after the war was 210.64 m.p.h. in September 1921, by a French Nieuport-Delage. By the end of the twenties, this figure had been almost doubled.

If you plot these absolute speed records in a simple chart form (shown below) you will see how keen was the competition to be fastest in the world after 1923. This was the era of the racing seaplane which remained the fastest form of vehicle throughout the twenties.

The Land Speed Records plotted on a separate line below, show how these lagged behind. By the time aircraft speeds were approaching the 300 m.p.h. mark, cars were still struggling to reach half this speed (yet 150 m.p.h. was the unofficially recorded speed of a Stanley Steamer car as far back as 1907!).

The obvious "target" figures were 300 m.p.h. for aircraft, and 200 m.p.h. on land. Strangely enough, these were both reached in 1927.

What other speed record figures can you discover for the twenties to plot on a separate line? Speed on water, for example? Or train speeds?

Subjects for wall-charts
Besides speed records, there are plenty of other achievements in the twenties for which you can make interesting wall charts. Instead of dividing the chart vertically into a speed scale, for example, mark this out as an altitude scale. A scale range of 35,000 to 45,000 feet will cover the altitude records of the twenties.

The record standing in 1920 was 35,433 ft., reached by two Germans in a hydrogen balloon in 1901. This was beaten by a Nieuport aircraft, flown by Lecointe (France) in 1923, when he reached a height of 36,565 ft. In 1927, Captain Gray of the U.S. reached 42,470 ft. in a balloon. See if you can unearth other aircraft altitude records for the twenties.

Another good chart subject is distance achieved

by aircraft, flying in a straight line, non-stop.

Athletics
Athletics records can also be plotted on a graph. Races such as the 100 yards will have to be plotted as times rather than speeds. You can easily convert record time into speed, using the appropriate formula given below:

For 100 yards, divide 200 by the time in seconds to give speed in m.p.h. For example, if the record time is 10 seconds, 200 divided by 10 = 20 m.p.h.

For 200 yards, divide 450 by time in seconds to give speed in m.p.h.

For 440 yards, divide 900 by time in seconds to give speed in m.p.h.

For 880 yards, divide 1800 by time in seconds to give speed in m.p.h. (Convert time in minutes and seconds into seconds.)

For 1 mile, divide 3600 by time in seconds to give speed in m.p.h. (Convert time in minutes and seconds into seconds.)

Note that the conversion for 100 yards is approximate. The other conversions are exact.

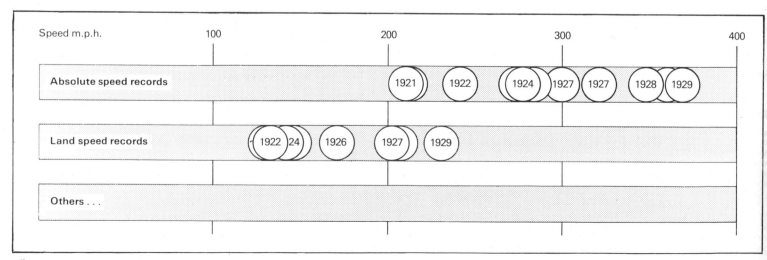

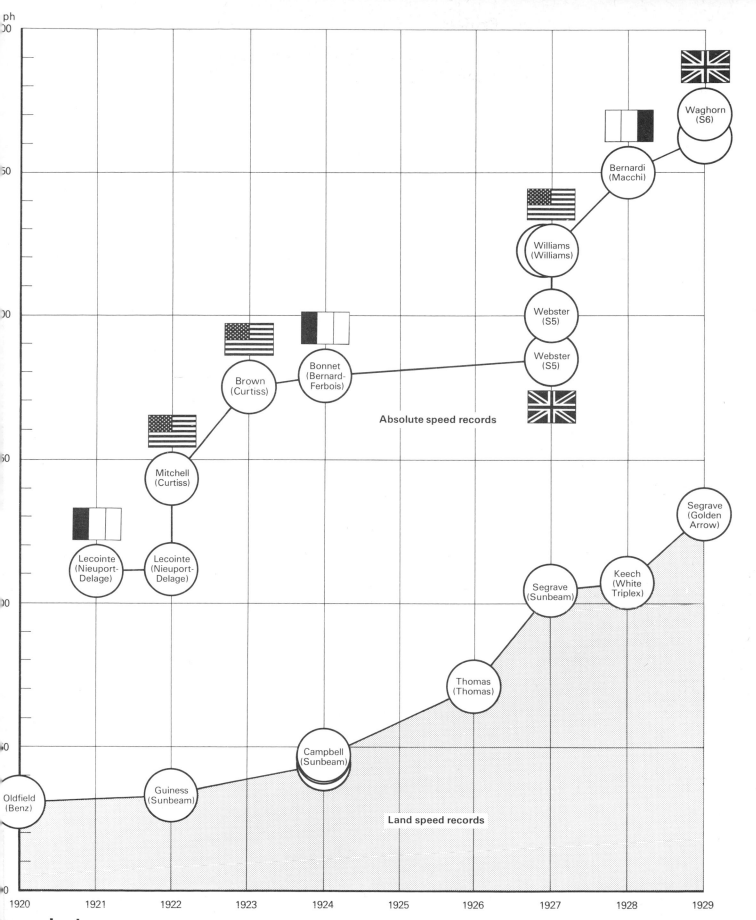

ph
00

50

00

50

00

50

00

50

00

Waghorn
(S6)

Bernardi
(Macchi)

Williams
(Williams)

Webster
(S5)

Webster
(S5)

Absolute speed records

Brown
(Curtiss)

Bonnet
(Bernard-
Ferbois)

Mitchell
(Curtiss)

Segrave
(Golden
Arrow)

Lecointe
(Nieuport-
Delage)

Lecointe
(Nieuport-
Delage)

Keech
(White
Triplex)

Segrave
(Sunbeam)

Thomas
(Thomas)

Campbell
(Sunbeam)

Oldfield
(Benz)

Guiness
(Sunbeam)

Land speed records

1920   1921   1922   1923   1924   1925   1926   1927   1928   1929

arge chart

you find that a simple chart like the one opposite
comes too crowded you could draw up a larger
art, like the one above. The larger the chart, the
re space you will have for recording details of
dividual records. Draw it up on a large sheet of
per which you can then paste to card, or a piece
hardboard, and hang up on a wall. After plotting
the various records you can fill the blank spaces
th cuttings or illustrations which you may be
le to find about individual record holders. You
uld even make cut-out models of individual record
lders (as described on pages 56-7) to stick to the

chart.

All the records given in the two lists on this page
are shown plotted on the sample chart opposite.
Each record is marked by a circle, centred on the
year and speed figures. You can draw these circles,
or cut them out from coloured paper and stick them
on. Print on neatly brief details of the record, and add
a national flag. This can be drawn on the chart, or on
a separate piece of paper, cut out and mounted on
a pin stuck into the circle. Join up the record points
and you will have a complete graph of the progress
of speed records—one for speed on land and one

for speed in the air.

To include other speed records you may need to
extend the speed scale downwards, but this is easily
done. You could add a separate plot of trans-Atlantic
liner record crossing speeds—another type of
record which was of considerable interest and
importance in the twenties.

You do not have to stick to "official" records. The
Guinness Book of Records gives 210 m.p.h. as the
speed reached by World War One fighters in dives,
for instance.

Making the tuning coils

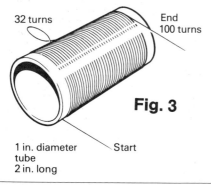

Fig. 2

32 turns

End
220 turns

1 in. diameter
card tube
2½ in. long

Start

Cut a 2½ in. length of the 1 in. diameter card tube. Now take the 38 gauge enamelled wire and start winding turns around the tube close to each other until you have completed 32 full turns (Fig. 2). At this point take a twist in the wire to form a loop, standing away from the coil, at least ½ in. long. Now continue winding on turns close to each other, until you have completed 220 turns.

Secure the beginning and end of the winding with a blob of sealing wax, then cut off the wire leaving a free length of about 2 in. at each end. Scrape the enamel off the last ½ in. of each wire end and also off the loop of wire, using a knife or fine glasspaper.

This completes the long wave coil. The medium wave coil (Fig. 3) is made in exactly the same way but this time winding on only 100 complete turns. The loop comes at the 32 turn point as before.

Fig. 3

32 turns

End
100 turns

1 in. diameter
tube
2 in. long

Start

In this project, you can find out how to make a simple radio set, and also how to experiment with it to get the best results.

Crystal sets are the simplest of all types of radio receivers—and the earliest. They use very few components, are easy to construct, and do not need a battery to operate them.

There are, however, snags. The signal picked up by a crystal set is very weak, and can only be heard through earphones. Signals from distant stations will be too weak to be heard at all.

But most sets, if built properly, with a good aerial and earth, should be able to pick up at least one or two stations, and in some parts of the country, even more.

The components which are used to make a crystal set are shown in Fig. 1. These are:

A variable capacitor or tuning control, by means of which the set can be tuned to different broadcasting stations.

A tuning coil which determines the "band" over which the set can be tuned. Two coils need to be made: one for tuning into the long wave band and another for tuning into the medium wave band.

A diode which actually detects the signal and turns it into a form which can be heard through earphones. In the twenties radio receivers used a quartz crystal and a "cat's whisker" as a detector. The modern diode does the same job more conveniently, and more efficiently.

Capacitor 1 which connects across the "phones" and improves the quality of the signal.

Capacitor 2 through which the **aerial** is connected to the tuning coil.

All these are standard components which can be bought from any radio spares shop. The tuning coils are easily made, rather than bought, which will reduce the cost of the components required (exclusive of earphones) to a few pence. The earphones you require are high impedance type (ask for 10,000 ohms impedance). You should be able to buy a pair for about 50p. Alternatively you can use a deaf-aid earpiece (impedance about 7,500 ohms).

Fig. 1 shows the position and shapes of the various components, and also how they are connected to complete the crystal set circuit.

Step 1 (Fig. 4)
Cut a base panel 4½ in. × 3 in. from ⅛ in. or 3/16 in. ply of Paxolin sheet. Mark out the position of the holes A, B, C, D and E as shown and drill with a 3 mm. or ⅛ in. drill.

Step 2 (Fig. 5)
A 6BA brass bolt is then fitted in each hole, as shown, using a washer on each side of the base and a nut tightened up to hold the bolt in position. Mark

the identifying letters A, B, C, D and E on the base as a guide for connection points later on.

Step 3 (Fig. 6)
Mount the variable capacitor on the base between bolts A and B. Stick it down with a contact adhesive. You may find that the component you have bought has a bolt protruding from the bottom. In this case, drill a hole in the base to take this bolt and secure in place with a nut.

The variable capacitor will have two terminal tags. These may be at opposite ends, or both at one end, or on one side. It does not matter which. All you have to remember is that one tag has to be connected to bolt A and the other tag to bolt B using a short length of flexible wire. To complete step 3, connect bolt A to bolt D with a further length of flex.

Step 4 (Fig. 7)
The diode has a thin wire emerging from each end. Straighten each wire out carefully and mount the diode between bolts C and E as shown. Identify capacitor 1 by the value marked on it (either .001 microfarad or just .001). Connect between bolts D and E, using the wires emerging from the ends of the component. Cut off surplus wire neatly.

Now connect the other capacitor between bolts C and F in the same way. Cut off surplus capacitor lead wire.

Step 5 (Fig. 8)
Lay the coil on the base, alongside the variable capacitor. Run a nut onto bolt C and position the coil so that the loop of bared wire can be slipped over bolt C. Add a second nut to secure the wire loop and complete connection to bolt C.

The start end of the coil winding is then connected to bolt A, using a nut to hold it in place and complete the connection. The finish end of the coil winding is connected to bolt B in a similar way.

Note that none of the coil winding connections should be soldered. Use nuts to hold the wires in place. This enables you to change coils.

Step 6 (Fig. 9)
Your crystal set can then be completed by connecting an aerial wire to bolt F; earphones to bolts D and E; and connecting bolt A to a good earth.

For the aerial, use as long a length of wire as you can and lead it away from the set in a vertical direction.

For the earth point, choose a water pipe or a hot-water radiator. Lead a wire from bolt A on the set of this "earth" and make sure that this connects to clean bare metal on the earthing point.

Fig. 1
Components to buy

Variable capacitor—500 picafarad mica compression trimmer, or equivalent miniature component.
Diode—any germanium crystal diode will do, or you can ask for a GEC GEX34 or equivalent.
Capacitor 1—.001 microfarad capacitor.
Capacitor 2—220 picafarad capacitor.

You will also need the following:
About 100 feet of 36 or 38 gauge enamelled copper wire (for winding the tuning coils). Thin flexible insulated wire for some connections, also for the aerial wire and earth connection. Six 6BA brass bolts, 12 nuts, and 12 washers. A 1 in. diameter card tube about 6 in. long. A panel 4½ in. × 3½ in. of Paxolin or plywood for the base.

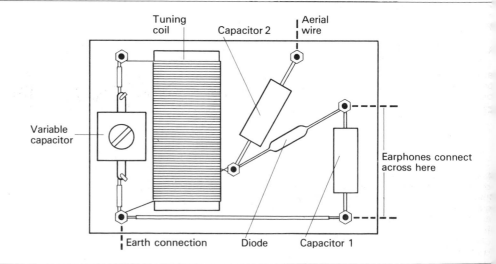

Tuning coil | Capacitor 2 | Aerial wire

Variable capacitor

Earphones connect across here

Earth connection | Diode | Capacitor 1

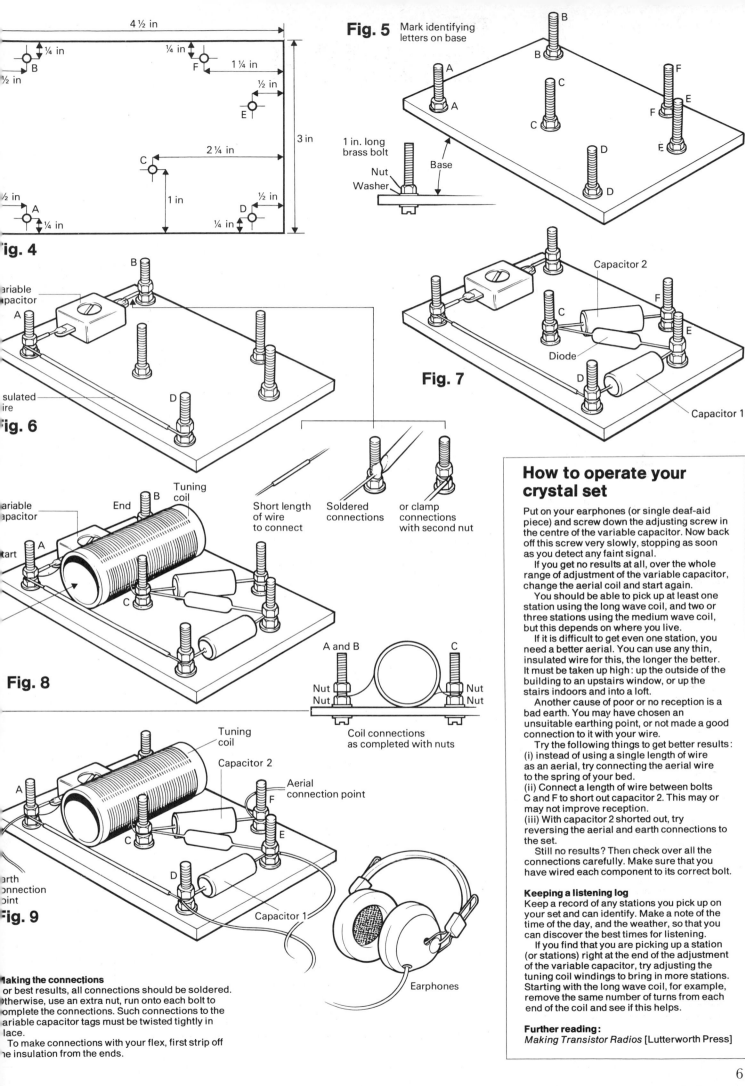

Fig. 4

4 ½ in

¼ in
B
¼ in
F
1 ¼ in
½ in
½ in
E
½ in
C
2 ¼ in
3 in
1 in
½ in
½ in
A
D
¼ in
¼ in

Fig. 5 Mark identifying letters on base

B
B
A
A
C
C
F
F
E
E
D
D

1 in. long brass bolt
Nut
Washer
Base

Fig. 6

Variable capacitor
A
B
Insulated wire
D

Fig. 7

Capacitor 2
C
F
E
Diode
D
Capacitor 1

Short length of wire to connect
Soldered connections
or clamp connections with second nut

Fig. 8

Variable capacitor
Start
End
Tuning coil
B
A
C
D

A and B
Nut
Nut
C
Nut
Nut
Coil connections as completed with nuts

Fig. 9

Tuning coil
Capacitor 2
Aerial connection point
A
F
C
E
Earth connection point
D
Capacitor 1
Earphones

How to operate your crystal set

Put on your earphones (or single deaf-aid piece) and screw down the adjusting screw in the centre of the variable capacitor. Now back off this screw very slowly, stopping as soon as you detect any faint signal.

If you get no results at all, over the whole range of adjustment of the variable capacitor, change the aerial coil and start again.

You should be able to pick up at least one station using the long wave coil, and two or three stations using the medium wave coil, but this depends on where you live.

If it is difficult to get even one station, you need a better aerial. You can use any thin, insulated wire for this, the longer the better. It must be taken up high: up the outside of the building to an upstairs window, or up the stairs indoors and into a loft.

Another cause of poor or no reception is a bad earth. You may have chosen an unsuitable earthing point, or not made a good connection to it with your wire.

Try the following things to get better results:
(i) instead of using a single length of wire as an aerial, try connecting the aerial wire to the spring of your bed.
(ii) Connect a length of wire between bolts C and F to short out capacitor 2. This may or may not improve reception.
(iii) With capacitor 2 shorted out, try reversing the aerial and earth connections to the set.

Still no results? Then check over all the connections carefully. Make sure that you have wired each component to its correct bolt.

Keeping a listening log
Keep a record of any stations you pick up on your set and can identify. Make a note of the time of the day, and the weather, so that you can discover the best times for listening.

If you find that you are picking up a station (or stations) right at the end of the adjustment of the variable capacitor, try adjusting the tuning coil windings to bring in more stations. Starting with the long wave coil, for example, remove the same number of turns from each end of the coil and see if this helps.

Further reading:
Making Transistor Radios [Lutterworth Press]

Making the connections
For best results, all connections should be soldered. Otherwise, use an extra nut, run onto each bolt to complete the connections. Such connections to the variable capacitor tags must be twisted tightly in place.

To make connections with your flex, first strip off the insulation from the ends.

Index

Note: Numbers in bold refer to illustrations or maps.

Abd el Krim, 46, **46**, 52-3
Achimota college, 46
advertising, **7**, 36-7, **36-7**, 44
aeroplanes, see aviation
Africa, 46-7, **46-7**
agriculture; in U.S., 14; in India, **16**; in Russia, 32-3, **32-3**; in Africa, 46; world, 48
aircraft, see aviation
airmail services, 11, **11**
airships, 10, **10**, 53
Alcock, Capt. John, first to cross Atlantic in an aeroplane, 10, 52
alcohol, see prohibition
Aldington, R., novelist, 50, 53
Alexander I, King of Yugoslavia, 53
Alfonso XIII, King of Spain, 55
Algeria, 47
America, see United States
Amritsar Massacre, 16-17, 52
anarchists, 14
Anglo-Persian Oil Company, 23, **23**
Angola, 47
d'Annunzio, Gabriel, Italian nationalist 18, **18**, 52
"anti-art", see Dadaism
antibiotics, 35
Anti-Saloon League, 42
apartheid, 53
Appleton, Sir E.V., scientist, 53
Arabs, 22-3, 51, 53
Arbuckle, Fatty, film comedian, 40
archaeology, 35, **35**
architecture, 24-5, **25**, 52-3
Armstrong, Louis, jazz musician, 15, 24, 53
army, Indian, 17, **17**
Arsenal football club, 30, **30**
arts, see painting, music, drama, architecture, literature, poetry, sculpture
Asia; Central, 7, 23, 27-9, 49; East, 17, see also China, Japan; Southern, 11, 25, 27; South-East, 11, 27
Astor, Lady, first British woman M.P., 52
astronomy, 53
Atlantic, crossing of, see aviation
atom bomb, 34
atomic scientists, 34, 52, 55
Austin, Herbert, car manufacturer, 20-1
Austin Seven, 7, 20-1, 56
Australia; flights to, 10-11, 53; cars in, 20; sport, 30-1; parliament, 53
Austria, 9, 52
Austria-Hungary, 4
aviation, 10-11, **10-11**, **53**

Baird, John Logie, 44, **44**, 53-4
Baldwin, Stanley, British prime minister, 52-4
Banting and Best, Canadian scientists, 35
Bara, Theda, 40
Bartok, B., composer, 24, 52-3
baseball, 30, **30**
Basutoland, 47
bathing costumes, 7, **7**, 37, 31
Battleship Potemkin, 40, 54
Bauhaus, the, 24-5, **25**, 52-3
Bavaria, 28-9
Beach, Sylvia, 50-1, **50**
Bechuanaland, 47
Beer Hall Putsch, see Munich Putsch
Bela Kun, Hungarian leader, 4, 52
Belfast, see Ireland
Belgium, 4, 26, **26**, 46-7
Belloc, Hilaire, poet, 50, 52
Bennett, Arnold, novelist, 50-1
Bentley car, 20
Berlin, **5**, 7, 24, see also Munich Putsch, Kapp Putsch
Bernhardt, Sarah, actress, 52
birth control, 6
Black and Tans, 52
black population in U.S., 14-15
blood transfusion and groups, 35
Bloomsbury group, 51
Bocage, scientist, 35

Bohr, Niels, scientist, 34
Bolshevik, see Communist
Bonar Law, Andrew, British prime minister, 52, 54
Bondfield, Margaret, first British woman Cabinet member, 53
"bootleg" liquor, see prohibition
Borotra, tennis player, 30
boxing, 30-1, **31**
Braque, G., artist, 53
Brecht, Berthold, 24, 53
Briand, Aristide, French premier, 54, **54**
Britain; post-war, 4, 12; and Russian Civil War, 8; labour unrest in, 12-13, **13**; in India, 16-17, **17**; and German reparations, 26; and China, 38; in Africa, 46-7, **47**; the Depression in, 49; see also the vote, cars, aviation, the Middle East, sport, cinema, newspapers, radio, theatre
British Broadcasting Company (B.B.C.), 44, 52-3
British Miners' Federation, 13
British Petroleum, 23
broadcasting, see radio
Broadway musicals, see Gershwin
Brooklands race track, **20**, 31
Brown, pilot, see Alcock
Bugatti, Type 35 and Ettore Bugatti, 31, **31**
Bushman, Francis X, film actor, 41
Byrd, R. E., pilot, 10, 53-5

Cadillac car, 43
Calcutta (India), **17**
California, 40
Cameroons, 47
Campbell, Malcolm, 20
Canberra (Australia), 53
Canton (China), 38
Capone, Al, Chicago gangster, 43, **43**, 53, **53**
Carnarvon, Lord, 35
cars, **cover**, 3, 7, **7**, 14, 20-1, **20-1**, 36, **41**, 52; racing, 20, 30-1, **31**
Carter, Howard, archaeologist, 35
cartoons, see cinema, Walt Disney, Mickey Mouse
censorship, in Italy, 18
Chanak, 22
Chaplin, Charlie, 36, **36**, 40-1, **40-1**, 52-3, **52**
Charleston, the, 3, **7**, see also dancing
Chelsea football club, 30, **30**
Chesterton, G. K., novelist and poet, 50
Chiang Kai-shek, president of Republic of China, 38-9, **39**, 53-4, **53**
Chicago, **7**, 42-3, 53
China, 38-9, **39**, 52-4
Chingkangshan, 39
Chou En-lai, 38
cinema, 3, 6, 40-1, **40-1**, 52-3; in U.S., 14, 36; in Germany, 24-5, **25**; in Europe, 36, **36**; see also film stars
Citroen car, 7, 20
civil disobedience, in India, 16-17, 54
Clemenceau, Georges Eugène, premier of France, 52, 55
coal industry; in Britain, 12-13, **12-13**; as a fuel, 23, 26; in Russia, 32, **32**
Cobham, Alan, British pilot, 10-11, **11**, 53-4, **53**
Cochet, tennis player, 30
Cockroft, and Walton, scientists, 34
collectivism, in Russia, 32, **32**, 53
colonial rule; India, 16-17; Africa, 46-7, **46-7**
Comintern, 52, see also Communism
Commonwealth, the, 30, 53
communications, see radio, television, newspapers, magazines
Communism; in Hungary, 4; and trade unionists, 12-13, **13**; in Germany, **12**, 28; in U.S., 14; in Italy, 18; in China, 38-9, **39**; see also Russia, International
Congo, Belgian, 47
Conklin, Chester, film comedian, 40
Conrad, Joseph, novelist, 53
Conservative Party (Britain), 52, 55
Coogan, Jackie, film actor, **40**
Cook, A. J., British trade unionist, 13, **13**
Coolidge, Calvin, President of U.S., 14, 52-4
Coward, Noel, playwright, 37
cricket, 30-1, **31**

crime, see gangsters
crystal radio set, see radio
Cubism, 24
current affairs, see newspapers, magazines
Curzon Line, Poland's eastern frontier, 9

Dadaism, 24, 52
Daily Mirror, 36
Daily Sketch, 36
Dali, Salvador, artist, 24, **24**
dancing, 3, 6-7, **6-7**, **15**, 36
Dawes Plan, 26, 53, 55
Deeping, Warwick, novelist, 50
Delhi (India), **17**
Democritus, Greek thinker, 34
Dempsey, Jack, boxer, 31, **31**
Denikin, White leader (Russia), 8
Depression, the Great, 3, 48-9, **49**
design, 24-5, **25**, 35, 52
De Valera, Eamon, Sinn Fein leader, 53
devaluation, see Germany: economy
diabetes, 35, 52
disease, see medicine
Disney, Walt, 40, 53
doctors, see medicine
Douglas biplane, 10
drugs, see medicine

economics; post-war, 3-5, **5**; African, 46; see also Wall St. Crash, and individual countries
education; in Germany, 24; in Africa, 46; in Turkey, 54
Egypt, 22-3, 35-6, 46-7, 52-3
Einstein, Albert, 34, 53
Eisenstein, Sergei Mikhailovich, film director, 40, 54
electrons, 34
Eliot, T. S., poet, 50, 52
entertainment, see cinema, radio, dancing, cars, sport, newspapers, magazines
Epstein, Jacob, sculptor, 53
Ernst, Max, 24
Essen, 26, **27**
Ethiopia, 47
Europe, post-war, 4-7, **4-7**, 52; see also individual countries, cars, economics, industry, Locarno Pact

Fairbanks, Douglas, film actor, 36, 40, 52-3
Falla, M. de, composer, 52
famine, in Russia, 32-3, **33**
Fascism; in Italy, 3, 18-19, **18-19**, 52-3; in Spain, 55; see also Mussolini
fashion, **3**, 6-7, **7**, 35-7, **37**, **42**
Feisal, King of Iraq, 22
Ferber, Edna, novelist, 53
Fianna Fail party, 53, see also Ireland
films, see cinema, film stars
film stars, 36-7, **36-7**, 40-1, **40-1**
Finland, 4
Firpo, Battling, boxer, 31, **31**
Fitzgerald, Scott, novelist, 50, **50**, 53
Fiume, port of, 18, 52
Five-Year Plan (Russia), 32, 53
Flaherty, writer, 52
"flappers", 6, **6**, 53, see also women, vote
Fleming, Alexander, scientist, 35, **35**, 53
Fleming, Professor John, inventor, 44
football, 30, **30**
Ford, Ford Madox, novelist, 51, **51**
Ford, Henry, car manufacturer, 7, 20-1
Ford, Model T ("Tin Lizzie"), 20-1, **20-1**, 53
Forster, E. M., novelist, 53
Fourteen Points, 22, see also Wilson
Fourth of May Movement, 38-9, **39**
France; relations with Germany and the Ruhr, 3, 26-7, **26-7**, 54; post-war, 4; and Russian Civil War, 8; trade unions in, 12; colonies, 46-7; Depression, in 49; main events, 52-3; see also cars, Middle East
Fuad I, King of Egypt, 22, 52
furniture, see design

Galsworthy, John, novelist, 50-1
Gandhi, M. K., 16-17, **16-17**, 52-4
gangsters, 3, 42-3, **43**, see also Al Capone
Garbo, Greta, film star, 36, 40, 53

Gecaphone radio, 45, **45**
George V, King of England, 52
General Motors, 20
General Strike (Britain), 12-13, **13**, 53-4; (India), 16
German People's Party, 55
Germany; post-war economy, 3, 5, **5**, 26, 48, 53; relations with France and the Ruhr, 3, 26-7, **26-7**, 54; colonies, 4, 46; and Poland, 9; labour unrest, 12; arts, 24-5; the Depression, 49; flappers, **53**; main events, 52-3
Gershwin, George, composer, 24, 53-4, **54**
Gish, Lillian, film star, 40
Glasgow, 4
Goering, Hermann, German Nazi, 54
Gold Coast, 46-7
golf, 30
Graf Zeppelin, airship, **10**, 53
gramophone records, 24
Greece, 22, 52-4
Gropius, Walter, designer, 24, 52

Handley Page, aircraft company, 11
Harding, Warren, 52, 55
de Havilland aircraft, **11**
health, see medicine
Hemingway, Ernest, novelist, 50-1, **50**, 53
Hindenburg, Paul Ludwig, President of Germany, 53-4
Hindus, in India, 16-17, 52, see also Gandhi
Hinkler, aviator, 10
hire-purchase, 14
Hitler, Adolf, 28, **28**, 52-4, **52**
Hobbs, Jack, cricketer, 31, **31**
Hoffman, Alfred, U.S. trade unionist, 13, **13**
holidays, 20, 36-7, **37**
Hollywood, 40
Honegger, A., composer, 52
Hoover, Herbert, President of U.S., 49, **49**, 53
horse-racing, **3**, 30
Horthy, Admiral, Hungarian Regent, 5
housing, 12
Hungary, 4, 52
Huxley, Aldous, writer, 50, 52

immigration, to U.S., 14
Imperial Airways, 10
imperial powers, see colonial powers
independence, in Africa, 46-7
India, 16-17, **16-17**, 22, 52-3
industry and technology, 24; in Russia 32, **32**, 53; in Africa, 46
inflation, 3, 5, 5, 26, 28
influenza epidemic, 4, **4**
insulin, 35
International, the Communist, 4
Iraq, 22-3
Ireland, 4, **4**, 52-3, **52**, see also Lloyd George
Istanbul, 22
Italy; Fascism in, 3, 18-19, **18-19**, 52-3; labour unrest in, 12; sport, 30-1; colonies, 47; main events, 52-3; see also Middle East

Japan; and Russian Civil War, 8; labour unrest in, 12; military expenditure, 38, 52; population, industry, relations with China, 38
jazz, 3, 14-15, **15**, 24-5, **25**, 52, 54
Jews, 22, 28, 53, see also Nazis
John, Augustus, artist, 53
Jolson, Al, film star, 40, **40**, 53
Jones, Bobby, golfer, 30
Joyce, James, novelist, 50-2, **51**

Kafka, Franz, novelist, 50, 53-4
Kahr, Gustav von, German politician, 28
Kapp Putsch (Germany), 4, 52
Keaton, Buster, 40
Kellog-Briand Pact, 53
Kelly, Lt., aviator, 10
Kemal, Mustafa (later known as Kemal Ataturk), 22, **22**, 52-4, **54**
Kenya, 47
Kern, Jerome, composer, 53
Keystone Company, film-makers, 40-1, **41**
Kiev (Ukraine), 8, 55
Kingsford Smith, aviator, 10, 53
Klee, Paul, 24, **24**, 52-3

K.L.M., Dutch airline, 10
Kodaly, Z., composer, 52
Kolchak, White leader (Russia), 8
Kronstadt Rising, 32, 52
Ku Klux Klan, 14, **14**
Kuomintang, 38-9, 53-5, *see also* China

labour, 12-13, **12-13**, *see also* unemployment, trade unions
Labour Party (Britain), 53, 55
Lancia car, 20, **20**
Lang, Fritz, film director, 24-5, 53
Lateran Treaties, 53
Lausanne, Treaty of, 52
Lawrence, D. H., novelist, 50-2, **51**
Lawrence, T. E., novelist ("Lawrence of Arabia"), 51, **51**, 53
League of Nations, 22, 52-3, 55
Lebanon, 22
Le Corbusier, architect, 53
Leger, Fernand, artist, 24, **24**
Lemaitre, astronomer, 53
Lenin, Nicolai (pseud. of Vladimir Ilyich Ulyanov), Russian Communist leader, 8, 32-3, **33**, 52-3, 53, 55
Lewis, Sinclair, novelist, 50-2, **51**
Liberal Party (Britain), 55
Liberia, 47
libraries, 50
Libya, 47
Life magazine, 36, **36**
Lincoln car, **43**
Lindbergh, Charles, first solo flight over Atlantic, 10, **10**, 53, 55
liquor, *see* prohibition
literary magazines, *see* literature
literature, 36, 50-3
Lloyd, Harold, film star, 40-1, **41**
Lloyd George, David, British prime minister, 52, 54-5, **55**
Locarno Pact, 26, 53, 55
London, 7, 37, **37**
Ludendorff, Erich von, German general, 28, **28**, 54
Lugard, Lord, 46

Macdonald, Ramsey, British prime minister, 53-5
Macready, Lt., aviator, 10
Mafia, the, 43, **43**
magazines, 36, 51
Maginot Line, 53
Makerere college, 46
malnutrition, 14
Manchu Emperors, 38
Manchuria, 38
mandates; in Middle East, 22, 52; in Africa, 46-7
Mann, Thomas, novelist, 53
Mao Tse-tung, 38-9, **39**, 53
March on Rome, 18, **18**, 52, **52**, 55
Marconi, G., inventor, 44-5, **44**
mark, German, *see* inflation
Matteotti, Italian Socialist leader, 53
Maugham, Somerset, novelist, 37
medicine, 35, **35**, *see also* influenza, diabetes, vaccination
Mein Kampf, 28, 54
Melba, Dame Nellie, singer, 44, **44**, 52
Mercedes car, 20
Mesopotamia, excavations in, 35
Mickey Mouse, 40, 53, **53**
Milan (Italy), 18
Millet's crystal radio, 45, **45**, *see also* radio
miners and mining; in Britain, 12-13, **12-13**, 52-3; in South Africa, 46
missionaries, 46
Modigliani, A., artist, 52
Mondrian, Piet, artist, 24, **24**
money, *see* economics
Moore, Henry, sculptor, 53
Morocco, 46-7, 52-3
Morris, "bull nosed", **20**
Morris, W. R. (Lord Nuffield), car manufacturer, 20-1
Morris Minor, 7, **21**
Morse code, 44
Morton, Jelly Roll, 15, 24-5, **25**, 53
Moscow (Russia), 4
Moslems, in India, 16-17, 52
Mosul (Iraq), 22-3
motor racing, *see* cars
Mottram, novelist, 50
Mozambique, 47
Munich Putsch, 28-9, 52, 54
Munthe, E., novelist, 50
murder, *see* gangsters

music, 24, 52-4, *see also* jazz, dancing, musichall
musichall, 36
Muslims, in India, 16-17; Turkey, **22**, 54
Mussolini, Benito, Italian dictator, 18-19, **18-19**, 52-3, **52**, 55, **55**

Nanking (China), 53
Nash, Paul, artist, 53
nationalism; in India, 17; in Italy, 18; in Germany, 28; in China, 38-9, **39**; in Africa, 46-7, **46**; in Ireland, 52; *see also* individual countries
nationalization, in Britain, 12-13
National Playing Fields Association, 30
National Socialist German Workers' Party, *see* Nazis
Navarro, Ramon, film actor, 41
Nazis, 28, **28**, 54, *see also* Hitler
neo-plasticism, 24
New Economic Policy (Russia), 32, 52, 55
New Orleans, 15
newspapers; in U.S., 14, **43**; sport in, 30; in Britain, 36, 44-5
Newton, Isaac, 34
New York Stock Exchange, 3, 48-9, **49, 54**
New Yorker, the, 36
Nigeria, 47
night-clubs, 37, **37**
Nilbo, Fred, film director, 41
"normalcy", U.S. policy, 14
Northern Ireland, 4
Norway, 52
nuclear physics, 34, 52
Nyasaland, 47

O'Banion, Dion, gangster, 43
O'Casey, Sean, dramatist, 53
October Revolution, *see* Russia
oil and oilfields, 22-3, **22-3**
Oliver, King, jazz musician, 24
Ory, Kidd, jazz musician, 24
Owen, Wilfred, poet, 52

painting, 24, **24**, 52-3
Palestine, 22, 52-3
Paris, 7, 24, 52-3, **50**
Paulesco, Nicholas, scientist, 35
peace treaty, *see* World War One
peasants; Russian, 8-9, 32-3, **32-3**; Chinese, 39, **39**
Peking (China), 53
penicillin, 35, **35**, 53
pensions (Britain), 53
People's National Party, *see* Kuomintang
Petrograd (Leningrad, Russia), 8
petrol, 20, **20**
Peugeot car, 20-1, **21**
Philips radio, 45, **45**
physics, *see* Rutherford, Cockroft and Walton
Picasso, Pablo, 24, 52-3
Piccadilly Circus, **37**
Pickford, Mary, film star, 36, 40, 52
Pilsudski, Josef, President of Poland, 4, 8-9, **9**, 53, 55
Pirandello, L., dramatist, 52
poetry, 50, 52
Poincaré, Raymond, French premier and president, 26, **26**, 53, 55, **55**
Poland; post-war, 4; war with Russia, 4, 8-9, **8-9**, 52; cavalry, **9**; *see also* Pilsudski
police, in U.S., 42-3
poor, the, *see* poverty
Portugal, 46-7, 53, 55
Pound, Ezra, poet, 50-1
poverty; in U.S., 14, **48**; in Italy, 18
Priestley, J. B., novelist, 50, 53
prohibition, 14, 42-3, **42**, 50, 52; in Norway, 52
Prokofiev, S., composer, 53
protons, 34
Proust, Marcel, novelist, 50-1, **51**
Public Enemy Number One, 43
Puccini, G., composer, 53

racial intolerance, 14, 28
radio, 3, 14, 30, 36, 44-5, **44-5**, 52, 54; project, 60-1
railways, **9**, 12
Rapallo, Treaty of, 52
Ravel, M., composer, 53

Red Army (Chinese), 39, 53
Red Army (Russian), 8, **8**
Red Cross, the International, 33
Red Hot Peppers, the, jazz group, 25, **25**, *see also* Jelly Roll Morton
Reds, *see* Communism, Red Army
Reinhardt, theatre producer, 24
relativity, theory of, 34
religion, 46, *see also* Hindu, Muslim
Remarque, E. M., novelist, 50
Renoir, P. A., artist, 24
reparations, German, 4, 26, 52-3, 55
Revolution, the, *see* Russia, China
Rhodesia, 46-7
rich, the; Europe, **3**, 7, 20; U.S., 13, **48**; 36-7, **37**
Riga, Treaty of, 9
Rittweiger, Otto, designer, 25, **25**
Rivera, Primo de, dictator of Spain, 52, **54**, 55
roads, 20
Robertson, scientist, 35
Roehm, Ernst, German Nazi, 54
Roentgen, W. K., X-rays, 35
Rolls-Royce car, 20
Roman Catholic Church, 18, 53
Ruhr, the, 3, 26-8, **26-7**, 52-3
Rumania, 52
Russia; Communism in, 3; Empire, 4; Revolution, 8, 38-9; Russo-Polish war, 4, 8-9, **8-9**; Civil War, 8-9, **8-9**, 32; general, 32-3, **32-3**, 52-3; *see also* archaeology, Lenin
Ruth, Babe, baseball star, 30, **30**
Rutherford, Ernest, physicist, 34, 52, 55
Ryan monoplane, 10, 55

Sacco and Vanzetti, U.S. anarchists, 14, **14**
Sahara, 47
St. Germain, Treaty of, 52
St. Valentine's Day Massacre, 53
Salazar, Antonio, Portugese politician, 53, 55, **55**
San Francisco, 44
"Sapper", author, 50
Saurrat, Albert, 46
Scapa Flow, German fleet scuttled, 52
Schneider Trophy, 53
science, 34-5, **34-5**
Schoenberg, A., composer, 53
Scopes, Johnny, trial of, 14, 53
Scotland, 30
sculpture, 52-3
Segrave, Sir Henry, 31, 53
self-determination of nations, 22
Sennet, Mack, film-maker, 41
Shantung, 38-9, 53
Shaw, George Bernard, dramatist, 37; 52
Shell Petrol Co., **back cover**, 23
Sheriff, R. C., dramatist, 53
Shostakovich, D., composer, 53
Siberia, excavations, 35
Sierra Leone, 47
Simon Commission, India, 53
Sinn Fein, 52, *see also* Ireland
Six, Les (Paris), composers, 52
skyscrapers, 14
Smith, Bessie, blues singer, 14, **14**
Smith, Capt. Ross, aviator, 10
soccer (Association Football), 30, **30**, 52
Socialists; in Russia, 8; in Italy, 18, 53; in Germany, 28; Austria, 53
South Africa, 46-7, 53
South America, 48
South West Africa, 47
Soviet Russia, *see* Russia
Spain, colonies of, 46-7, 52; *see also* Primo de Rivera
Spartacists, 5, **5**
sport, 30, 30-1, **30-1**
stocks and shares, *see* Wall St. Crash
Stalin, Joseph, Russian leader, 32, 53
Stein, Gertrude, novelist, 50-1
Strachey, Lytton, writer, 50, 52
Stravinsky, I., composer, 24, 53
Stresemann, Gustav, German statesman, 26, 28, **28**, 52, 54-5
Stroheim, Erich von, film-maker, 52
Sudan, 47
Suez Canal, 22
Sultan, Turkish, 22
Sumerian temple, excavation of, 35
Sunbeam car, 20, 31, **31**
Sun Yat-sen, President of Republic of China, 38-9, **39**, 53-5

surrealism, 24, 52-3
Syria, 22

Tanganyika, 47
television, 44, **44**, 54
temperance movement, 42
Tennessee, 13
tennis, 30
theatre, 24, 36-7, 52-3
Time magazine, 36, 52
Trades Disputes Act, Britain, 53
trade unions; in Britain, 4, 12-13, **13**, 53; in U.S., 13, **13**; in Italy, 18, 53
Trade Union Congress, Britain, 13
Transatlantic Review, the, 51
Transjordan, 22
transport, *see* railways, cars, aviation
Trotsky, Lev Davidovich, Russian leader, 8, 32, 52-3
tuberculosis, 53
Tunney, Gene, boxer, 31
Turkey; Empire, 4; 22-3, **22-3**, 52, *see also* Kemal
Tutankhamun, 35-6, **35**

Ukraine, 8, 52
Uganda, 46-7
unemployment; post-war, **2**, 3-5, **5**, 12; in Italy, 18; after the Crash, 48-9, **49**; in Britain, 52
Union of Soviet Socialist Republics (U.S.S.R.), 52, *see also* Russia
United States of America; post-war, 6-7, **6-7**, 13; and Russian Civil War, 8; labour unrest, 12-13, **13**; general, 14, **14**, 48-9, **48-9**, 54; and Middle East, 23; main events, 52-3; *see also* cars, literature, sport, cinema, magazines, radio, dancing, gangsters, prohibition
United Textile Workers Union, 13
Ur, city of, excavations, 35
Utrillo, M., artist, 53

vaccination, 35, 52-3
Valentino, Rudolf, film star, 36, 40-1, **41**, 52-3, 55
Vatican, the, 18
Versailles, Treaty of, 38-9, 52, **52**
vice syndicate, 43
Vickers Vimy bomber, 10
Victor Emmanuel III, King of Italy, 55
vitamins, 35, **35**
Vogue magazine, **front cover**, 36
Voisin car, **41**
vote, the, 6, 52-4

Wafd, Egyptian political party, 22
Wallace, Edgar, novelist, 50
Wall St. Crash, 48-9, **48-9**, 53
war, *see* World War One
warlords, *see* China
Warsaw, 8, 55
Washington, Treaty of, 52
Weill, Kurt, composer, 24
Weimar (Germany), 24, 52
Weimar Republic, 28, 52, *see also* Hitler, Stresemann
Wells, H. G., novelist, 51
Whiteman, Paul, jazz musician, 52, 54
Whites, the, *see* Russia: civil war
Wilder, Thornton, dramatist, 53
Williamson, Henry, novelist, 53
Wilson, Woodrow, President of U.S., 14, 22, 52, 55
wireless, *see* radio
Wittelsbach monarchy, 28
women, social position of, 3, 6-7, **6-7**, 52, **53**; in Turkey, 22
Woolf, Virginia, novelist, 50-1, **51,** 53
Woolley, Sir Leonard, archaeologist, 35
World War One; results of, 3-5, **5**, 48; peace treaty, 5, 8, 35, 51-2, 55; war novels, 50-1; *see also* Hindenburg, Wilson

X-rays, 35

Yale, Frank, Mafia chief, 43
Yeats, W. B., poet, 50
Young Plan, 53
Yudenich, Russian general (White Army), 8
Yuan, Chinese general, 55
Yugoslavia, 53

Zinoviev letter, 53

Further Reading

Available in the United States and Canada:

ALLEN, FREDERICK LEWIS. *Only Yesterday; An Informal History of the Nineteen-Twenties.* Harper, 1957.
The American Heritage History of the 20's and 30's. American Heritage, 1970.
BOARDMAN, FON W., JR. *America and the Jazz Age: A History of the 1920's.* Walck, 1968.
BURLINGAME, ROGER. *Henry Ford: A Great Life in Brief.* Knopf, 1955.
DANIELS, JONATHAN. *The Time Between the Wars; Armistice to Pearl Harbor.* Doubleday, 1966.
EHRMANN, HERBERT B. *The Case That Will Not Die: Commonwealth vs. Sacco and Vanzetti.* Little, 1969.
FITZGERALD, F. SCOTT. *The Great Gatsby.* Scribner, 1925. *Tender is the Night.* Scribner, 1934. *This Side of Paradise.* Scribner, 1920.
HADLOCK, RICHARD. *Jazz Masters of the Twenties.* Macmillan, 1965.
HEMINGWAY, ERNEST. *The Sun Also Rises.* Scribner, 1926.
HOFFMAN, FREDERICK J. *The Twenties; American Writing in the Post-War Decade.* Free Press, 1965.
LEIGHTON, ISABEL. *The Aspirin Age: 1919-1941.* Simon & Schuster, 1968.
LEWIS, SINCLAIR. *Babbitt.* Harcourt, 1922. *Main Street.* Harcourt, 1920.
The Life History of the United States, Vol. 10, War, Boom and Bust: 1917-1932. Time, 1964.
LINDBERGH, CHARLES AUGUSTUS. *The Spirit of St. Louis.* Scribner, 1953. *"We."* Putnam, 1927.
RUSSELL, FRANCIS. *The Shadow of Blooming Grove: Warren G. Harding in His Time.* McGraw, 1968.
SCOPES, JOHN T. and PRESLEY JAMES. *Center of the Storm; Memoirs of John T. Scopes.* Holt, 1967.
SINCLAIR, ANDREW. *The Available Man; The Life Behind the Masks of Warren Gamaliel Harding.* Macmillan, 1965.
SNOWMAN, DANIEL. *America Since 1920.* Harper, 1969.
This Fabulous Century, Vol. 3, 1920-1930. Time, 1969.

Available in Britain:

ABSALOM, R. N. L. *Mussolini and the Rise of Italian Fascism.* Methuen 1969.
ALLEN, K. *Exploring the Cinema.* Odhams. 1968.
BAILY, L. *B.B.C. Scrapbook,* Vol 2 1918–39. Allen & Unwin. 1969.
BRUCE, R. *Sun Yat-Sen.* Oxford. 1969.
DODDS, J. *Everyday Life in Twentieth Century America.* Batsford. 1966.
DONCASTER, I. *Social Change in Twentieth Century England.* Longman. 1968.
ELLIOTT, B. J. *Hitler and Germany.* Longman. 1966.
FITZGERALD, C. P. *Communism takes China.* Macdonald. 1971.
HADLOCK, R. *Jazz Masters of the Twenties.* Collier Macmillan. 1966.
HARSTON, K. *Yesterday.* Allen & Unwin. 1968.
HILL, B. J. W. *Cricket.* Blackwell. 1960.
HILL, B. J. W. *Football.* Blackwell. 1961.
INGLIS, B. *The Story of Ireland.* Faber. 1965.
KENYON, J. W. *Boxing History.* Methuen. 1961.
LEWIS, A. F. *Only Yesterday.* Harper & Row. 1957.
LINECAR, H. *Early Aeroplanes.* Benn. 1965.
MONTGOMERY, J. *The Twenties.* Allen & Unwin. 1970.
NEAL, E. *Lenin and the Bolsheviks.* Hulton. 1967.
ROBBINS, D. *Painting between the Wars.* McGraw-Hill. 1966.
ROBERTS, J. M. *Europe 1880–1945.* Longmans. 1967.
ROOKE, P. J. *The Wind of Change in Africa.* Blackie. 1967.
SEAMAN, L. C. B. *Life in Britain Between the Wars.* Batsford. 1970.
SINCLAIR, A. *Prohibition.* Faber. 1962.
SLIDE, A. *The Early American Cinema.* Zwemmer. 1970.
SWINNERTON, F. *The Georgian Literary Scene.* Hutchinson. 1969.
TREGIDGO, P. *The Story of the Motor Car.* Longman. 1971.
UNSTEAD, R. J. *Britain in the Twentieth Century.* Black. 1966.
WATSON, F. *Gandhi.* Oxford. 1969.
WYMER, G. *From Marconi to Telstar.* Longman. 1966.

Acknowledgements

Special Adviser
Dr J. M. Roberts, Fellow and Tutor in Modern History at Merton College, Oxford

Editor
Sue Jacquemier

Assistant Editor
Tim Healey

Project author
R. H. Warring p. 56-60

Cover picture: twenties fashion from *Vogue*.
Back cover: Shell petrol poster of 1929.

Note: in this book all foreign words, titles of books, films, songs, etc., are in *italics,* e.g. *A Farewell to Arms.*

If we have unwittingly infringed copyright in any picture or photograph reproduced in this publication, we tender our sincere apologies and will be glad of the opportunity, upon being satisfied as to the owner's title, to pay an appropriate fee as if we had been able to obtain prior permission.

We wish to thank the following individuals and organizations for their assistance and for making available material in their collections.

Key to picture positions:
(T) top; (C) centre; (L) left; (B) bottom; (R) right and combinations; for example, (TC) top centre

Associated Press p. 43(TL)
Bertarelli p. 36(BR)
Bibliothèque Nationale p. 27
Black Star, Fleet St. p. 38(L), 39 (TL)
BOAC p. 11(BL)
B.P.C. Library p. 38(L), 39 (TL)
Bradford City Library p. 7(BL)
British Film Institute p. 25(B), 41(TL)
British Petroleum Co. Ltd. p. 23(TR)
Charles Chaplin Inc. p. 52(L)
Communist Party Headquarters p. 13(BR)
Editions Rencontre p. 18(BR), 52
Galerie der Staat p. 15
Hulton Picture Library p. 5(TL), 6(BR), 7(TL), 7(BR), 11(TL), 16(BR), 17(TL), 17(BL), 22(BL), 39(BR), 44(TL), 44(BR), 53, 55(L), 55(C)
Illustrated London News p. 35(BL)
Institute of Social History, Amsterdam p. 5(TC), 12(R), 26(CL)
Iraq Petroleum Co. p. 23(L)
Jozef Pilsudski Institute p. 9(BR)
Keystone p. 46(TL)
King Features p. 7(TR), 14(TL), 40(R), 48(TL), 49(TL)
Kladderadatsch p. 53
Labour Party Library p. 2
Library of Congress p. 6(L), 21(B), 36(TL), 43(R), 49(BL)
Macdonald Educational Visual Books p. 10(R), 11(TR), 20(BR) (BL), 21(TL) (TR), 31(TR) (TL)
Mansell Collection p. 30(TL) (BL), 51
Melody Maker p. 25(BL)

M.G.M. p. 41(TR)
Museum of British Transport p. 12(L), 37(TR)
Novosti p. 8(TL), 9(BL), 33(BR)
Popperfoto p. 10(L), 28(B)
Portuguese State Office p. 55(R)
Press Association p. 55
Queen p. 36(BL)
Queen Mary's Hospital Medical School p. 35(CL), 35(TL)
Science Museum p. 45(TL), 45(BL), 45(BR)
Shell-Mex & B.P. Ltd. p. 23(B), Back cover
Simplicissimus p. 48(BL)
Sikorski Institute p. 8, 9(T)
Snark, p. 19, 24(TL)
Society for Cultural Relations p. 33(TL)
Sumati Morarjee Collection, India p. 16(L)
Syndication International p. 13(BL)
Tate Gallery—Spadem p. 24(BL) (BC) (BR)
Thames & Hudson Ltd. p. 32(R)
Ullstein p. 52
United Press International p. 13(TL), 43(CL) (BL)
Victoria & Albert Museum 20(TL)
Viollet, Roger p. 49(BC)
Vogue. Front cover
Whitney Museum of American Art p. 30-31
Wurttembergischer Kunstverein, Stuttgart p. 25(T) (CL)

Artists and photographers
Axelbank, Herman p. 8(BL)
Beach, Sylvia p. 50(L)
Gerson, Mark p. 25(T)
Gordon Davies, William p. 44(BL)
Jones, Max p. 14(BL)
Laporte, Renée p. 24(TL)
Morrison, George p. 4(BL), 52
Morangies, B. p. 26(CL)
Mrs. Bernard Moore p. 17(TR)
St. Barbe Baker, Richard p. 46(BL)